A

THE BREAKUP
IS A
Blessing

How Letting Go Leads You To The Love You Deserve

Love Like An IT Girl

Dedicated To The Woman Who's Ready To Stop Settling For Less And Start Demanding The Love She Deserves—This One's For You, Darling.

Table Of Contents

About The Author

Hi, I'm Tatiana Jerome, and I'm going to be blunt with you: love is not supposed to hurt. This journey of healing, self-love, and growth? It's not about sugarcoating things. It's about being real, raw, and facing the truth—even when it stings. I'm not here to tiptoe around your feelings. I'm here to shake things up, challenge the beliefs you've held onto, and wake you up to who you really are. This is your time to step into your power, and I'm not holding back.

After a breakup that I thought would break me, I realized that God didn't just save me—He redirected me. That pain wasn't a dead end; it was a blessing. It was a redirection to a version of myself I had been ignoring. Through that process, I learned something crucial that I'm going to repeat until it sinks in: **you are not here to settle.** You are not here to chase love or beg for someone else's approval. **You are here to stand in your power, recognize your worth, and demand the love that aligns with that.**

I've been there. And this isn't just about me—it's about you. That's why I wrote my first book, *Love Lost, Love Found*, to share the raw truth of how I moved through heartbreak and redefined what love means. Now, in this book, I've updated my message and tailored it directly to you. This isn't a one-size-fits-all guide—it's *your* guide to rediscovering your worth and shifting your mindset to become the woman you've always been meant to be.

You, my dear, are an IT Girl—a woman who knows her value, stands tall in her purpose, and doesn't apologize for the life she desires. IT Girl Luxury isn't just a brand I created—it's a movement, a way of living. It's about embracing your inherent worth, being unapologetic about your desires, and not settling for anything less than what aligns with your true self. It's about cultivating a life of luxury, not just in material things, but in self-love, respect, and boundaries.

But you're also a Queen. A Queen doesn't beg, chase, or settle. She is revered, she is honored, and she demands love that respects her for who she is, not for what she can give. So why am I referring to you as an IT Girl and a Queen? Because they are one in the same. The IT Girl mindset embodies everything that a Queen is—powerful, deserving, unwavering in her worth—and I want you to step into that energy throughout this book.

This book is a new beginning. It's designed to help you stop settling, stop accepting crumbs, and stop thinking you don't deserve the very best. My mission here is clear: by the end of this book, you will be standing tall in your worth, knowing exactly what you deserve in love, life, and everything in between. You'll no longer be hiding pieces of yourself. You'll be owning your power, reclaiming your peace, and building a life and love that reflect your highest self.

As you read through these pages, you'll find spaces for self-reflection, journaling prompts, affirmations, and thought-provoking questions. These aren't just words on a page; they're a part of your awakening. They're designed to make you dig deeper, challenge the lies you've been told, and remind you that you are a Queen, deserving of the love, respect, and happiness that align with your true worth.

So, let's be clear: **this is not about waiting for someone else to give you permission to shine.** It's about you finally claiming the life you deserve. It's about shifting from playing small to being unapologetically bold. And by the end of this book, you'll no longer be questioning your worth—you'll be embodying the Queen you already are.

Are you ready to start? Let's do this. Let's walk this journey together, unapologetically. Because when you love yourself first, everything else falls into place.

Who Are You?

This is your chance to write out how you currently see yourself. Who would you say you are? Who do you identify as? Write it all down here.

_____

_____

_____

_____

_____

_____

_____

_____

_____

_____

_____

_____

_____

_____

_____

_____

_____

_____

_____

_____

_____

_____

_____

How Did
We Get Here?

L ove isn't pain. Love isn't confusion. Love isn't a silent war you're fighting to win. Yet, here we are, pretending it's all part of the story. Why? Why has settling become the default? Why are we accepting relationships that leave us exhausted, disappointed, and questioning our worth? Oh yeah, this is exactly how we are starting off. We're getting right into it. This isn't just about him—it's about you, us. Why do we stay in places that shrink us when we know we deserve so much more? Let's talk about the things we don't say out loud. The lies we tell ourselves to avoid the truth: he isn't it, and we know it.

Here's the truth that's hard to admit. Love like this—one-sided, draining, and cyclical—isn't love at all. It's a habit. A fear of starting over. A belief that if we hold on just a little longer, he'll change, he'll see, he'll finally get it. But he won't. And deep down, that's understood. So why is it so hard to let go? Why do we cling to something that feels more like a cage than a connection? Because the alternative—being alone, starting fresh, risking the unknown—terrifies us more than the slow death of staying.

A Queen never chases. Let that sink in. Throughout history, Queens have been revered, protected, and fought for. Kingdoms rose and fell on the strength of a Queen's love and presence. Kings would go to war for their Queens, risking everything for the woman who held their heart. A Queen understood her worth—she never begged, never pleaded, and never accepted less than the respect, devotion, and loyalty that were her birthright. So, why are we, modern-day Queens, finding ourselves in relationships where we feel the need to convince someone of our value? Why are we settling for love that feels like a battle we're fighting alone?

The truth is, love—real love—isn't something you chase. It's not something you beg for. Love is an offering, a sacred exchange, where the right King moves heaven and earth for his Queen. Yet, here we are, caught in relationships, situationships, and unclaimed spaces where we're doing all the moving, all the sacrificing, and all the emotional labor. Let's call it what it is: it's beneath us.

Queens don't settle for comfort. Queens know that a King worth his crown will honor their love, not see it as a convenience. But somehow, too many of us have forgotten what love is supposed to feel like. Maybe it's because we've been sold a story that love requires endless struggle. Maybe it's because we've been told that if we're not fighting for love, it isn't real. But here's the truth: the right King will never make you fight alone. He will show up, unshaken and unwavering, because real love doesn't ask you to shrink yourself or diminish your light.

How Did We Get Here?
How did we get here? Yes, talking to each other like this (nice to meet you). But really how? Let's face it—settling. You settled. Let me define settling for you. Settling is staying in something that doesn't nourish your soul because the idea of being alone feels heavier than the reality of being mistreated. It's letting "good enough" take the place of "extraordinary" because convincing yourself to wait for potential is easier than facing the truth. Settling is what happens when we trade our happiness for someone else's

convenience. Settling isn't something that happens overnight. It starts small, so subtle you might not even notice. The missed calls, the empty promises, the way your needs slowly get pushed to the side. And instead of addressing it, you make excuses. "He's just busy." "He doesn't mean to hurt me." "Maybe I'm asking for too much." But you're not asking for too much. You're asking the wrong person. A King doesn't need to be reminded how to love his Queen.

Back then, when Queens walked through palaces and men bowed in their presence, love wasn't transactional. It wasn't a balancing act or a series of compromises. A King knew it was his privilege to honor her. And yet, today, we've convinced ourselves that love is something we have to hustle for, as if being loved is a prize we must earn. It's time to unlearn that lie.

Let's talk about love and what it truly feels like. Love doesn't leave you guessing. Love doesn't make you question your worth. Love feels like a fortress—strong, unwavering, and safe. It feels like a King standing beside his Queen, ready to fight the battles of life together. Love isn't found in breadcrumbs or potential; it's found in the actions that scream, "I choose you, every single day."

Let's talk more about how you got here. No, not the sanitized version—the real one. Maybe he was everything you thought you wanted in the beginning. Charming, attentive, a little too perfect. Or maybe you knew from the start that he wasn't right, but you stayed because you thought you could change him. It always starts small, doesn't it? He forgets an important date. He "jokes" about something you're insecure about. He makes promises he doesn't keep. And then, slowly but surely, you find yourself making excuses for him, lowering your standards piece by piece until you barely recognize yourself. Settling doesn't happen all at once—it's death by a thousand cuts.

Here's the truth no one wants to admit: potential is the most dangerous thing about a relationship. It's the carrot dangled in front of you, just close enough to keep you moving forward but always out of reach. You hold onto the idea of who he *could* be, who you *could* be together, while ignoring who he actually is and how he actually makes you feel. Potential is a lie you tell yourself when the reality is too painful to face. And it's time to stop lying. You must realize that potential keeps you in the waiting room of a love story that never actually begins. Queens don't wait on potential. They don't sit on thrones hoping their Kings will one day realize their worth. A Queen recognizes when it's time to leave the banquet table and write a new love story—one where she is the main character, the prize, the everything.

So why this book? And why now? Because it's time for a new narrative. Because too many of us are holding onto things that don't serve us. Too many of us are settling for half-love, for breadcrumbs, for relationships that feel like emotional gymnastics. And too many of us are too afraid to ask for more. Truth be told: the life and love you want are waiting for you. You just have to decide that you're ready to claim them. It's time to rewrite the story of love and relationships. This isn't just about romance—it's about reclaiming the power we've handed away in the name of love. It's about recognizing the difference between love and obligation, between partnership and convenience. This book is your reminder that you are a Queen, and IT Girl, and an Queen doesn't settle for less than a King.

What does that look like? It looks like redefining love on your terms. Setting boundaries that protect your peace. Letting go of people who don't value you. And most importantly, it looks like doing the hard work of loving yourself first. Because when you love yourself deeply, you stop accepting love that feels like pain.

Let's talk about what's next. In these pages, we're going to unpack it all. The lies we've been told about love. The stories we've internalized about what we're worth. The patterns we've fallen into and the ways to break free. We're going to talk about what love is supposed to feel like and how to recognize it when it shows up. We're going to talk about how to let go—of the pain, the past, and the person who wasn't it. And we're going to talk about how to move forward, stronger and more aligned with the love you deserve.

Let's get practical. Whether you're navigating the end of a relationship, questioning your marriage, or recovering from a situationship that left you feeling unclaimed, this book is your map back to yourself. It's the process of examining the red flags we've ignored, the compromises we've made, and the love we've been conditioned to accept. It's the bold decision to say no to the bare minimum and yes to everything you deserve.

This isn't just a book—it's a revolution. A call to arms for every woman who's ever felt like she was too much or not enough. A reminder that love starts with us and that the love you want begins with the love you give yourself. It's the transformation into the Queen, the IT Girl, who knows her worth, embraces her power, and attracts the King who will move mountains to stand beside her.

So, let's do this together. Let's let go of the past, embrace the present, and walk boldly into the future. Let's create a love life that feels as good as it looks. Let's become the IT Girls of our own stories. Because we're worth it. We've always been worth it.

Part 1:
Recognizing What Love Isn't

Remember When You Dreamed Of Forever?

It always starts with the dream. Remember when you imagined your love story as a symphony, one where the crescendos would echo through a lifetime? The fairytale felt real. He said all the right things, or maybe he said very little, and you filled in the blanks. It's easy to do that—to take silences as mystery, red flags as passion, and good-enough as love. So, what happened?

How did the symphony turn into static? When did you become the one orchestrating every note while he stopped showing up for the music? You many not want to think of it like this—who does? But if we're going to get real, and we absolutely should, it's time to face a hard truth: you've been playing all the roles in this love story. Lead, supporting actress, director, writer, costume designer, even craft services. You've done it all. And for what? A man who treats you like an understudy?

The Moment It Shifted

The shift is rarely an earthquake. It doesn't announce itself with sirens or bold declarations. It's subtle, sneaky—a quiet dismantling of what once felt like the most secure thing in your life. You can pinpoint the day he stopped saying, "I love you," but you can't quite pinpoint when he stopped meaning it. Maybe it was a single moment, or maybe it was a slow erosion. The realization creeps in, like noticing a plant you swore you watered is somehow wilting.

The shift is in the things you brush off. The unanswered text that lingers too long. The eye roll at your excitement. The way his touch feels absent, even when he's holding your hand. These tiny fractures seem harmless at first, until you step back and realize the foundation of your relationship is riddled with cracks.

The Things We Tell Ourselves

And yet, we stay. We tell ourselves stories to make it make sense. He's tired, he's stressed, he's just going through something right now. But deep down, we know. We know that love shouldn't feel like begging for crumbs. It shouldn't feel like reading between the lines of a text message to decipher if he still cares.

Remember the version of yourself who once vowed, "I'd never tolerate this." Where did she go? How did her boundaries blur into lines so faint you don't even know where they were drawn anymore? The moment it shifted wasn't just about him. It was about us, too. Because somewhere along the way, we started making excuses.

The Shift In Action

Has this happened (or something similar)? A dinner that's supposed to be special. You dress up, you plan, you show up full of hope that this night will feel like it used to. And yet, he spends the evening scrolling his phone, responding with one-word answers, and making you feel like an inconvenience rather than a priority. That's the shift. It's the moment you realize you're the only one still trying.

But acknowledging that shift is terrifying, isn't it? Because once you do, you can't go back to pretending everything is fine. You can't unsee the way he looks at you with indifference instead of love. You can't unfeel the loneliness of being with someone who no longer chooses you.

Why We Stay

Why do we cling to something that's breaking us? Fear. Fear of starting over, of the unknown, of being alone. Fear of looking foolish for investing so much into something that's crumbling. And there's no point in pretending, there's a part of us that hopes. Hopes that maybe, just maybe, things will go back to the way they were. That he'll wake up one day and remember how to love you the way he once did.

No filter, here it is: love shouldn't feel like a gamble. It shouldn't feel like a waiting game where you're always the one hoping for change.

Recognizing The Shift

So, how do you know when the shift has happened? Here are some signs:

1. **Emotional Disconnection:** The conversations that once flowed effortlessly now feel forced, or worse, non-existent.

2. **Physical Absence:** Even when he's there, it feels like he's not. His touch lacks warmth, his kisses lack intention.

3. **Dismissiveness:** Your feelings are minimized. He tells you you're "being dramatic" or "being too sensitive."

4. **Neglect:** You're no longer a priority. Plans are canceled, promises are broken, and effort is nowhere to be found.

5. **Loneliness:** You feel alone, even when you're together. It's a specific kind of loneliness that only

comes from being unseen by someone who once knew you best.

Facing The Shift

Acknowledging the shift is one of the hardest things you'll ever do. It requires brutal honesty with yourself. It means letting go of the stories you've been telling yourself to keep the peace. It's admitting that the person you love might not love you the way you deserve to be loved.

So What Should You Do If You Haven't Already?

Start With Self-Reflection: Below, space is provided for you to write it all out. What are you feeling? What moments stand out as signs of the shift? Sometimes, seeing your thoughts on paper brings clarity.

_____

_____

_____

_____

_____

_____

_____

_____

_____

_____

_____

_____

_____

_____

Here is a place for you to write out your thoughts

I Am Feeling:

_____

_____

_____

_____

_____

_____

_____

_____

_____

_____

_____

_____

_____

_____

_____

_____

_____

_____

_____

_____

I Am Tired Of Feeling:

_____

_____

_____

_____

_____

_____

_____

_____

_____

_____

_____

_____

_____

_____

_____

_____

_____

_____

_____

_____

_____

_____

_____

_____

_____

My Thoughts:

_____

_____

_____

_____

_____

_____

_____

_____

_____

_____

_____

_____

_____

_____

_____

_____

_____

_____

_____

_____

_____

_____

_____

_____

The False Comfort Of History

History is seductive. It whispers, *Remember how good it used to be?* It wraps itself around you like a warm blanket, convincing you to stay in a relationship that no longer serves you because of what it once was.

We romanticize the past, don't we? We replay the memories of the good times—the laughter, the passion, the connection. We tell ourselves, *If it was that good once, it can be that good again.* But here's the problem with history: it's a liar.

Just because he loved you then doesn't mean he loves you now. Just because he made you feel special once doesn't mean he's making you feel special today. And just because you've been together for years doesn't mean you're meant to stay together forever.

But we hold onto history because it feels safe. It feels familiar. It feels like proof that the relationship is worth fighting for. But at what cost? How much of yourself are you willing to sacrifice for a love that only exists in your memories?

Think about it: how many times have you justified staying because of the time you've already invested? How many times have you told yourself, *But we've been through so much together,* as if surviving hardship is the same as thriving in love?

Here's the truth: history is not a reason to stay. Love is not defined by what happened years ago. It's rooted in what's happening now. And if what's happening now isn't making you happy, fulfilled, and valued, then history is nothing more than a chain keeping you tied to something that's no longer serving you.

So, what do you do? You let go. You stop clinging to the past and start focusing on the present. You stop romanticizing what was and start creating space for what could be. Because history is a foundation, not a prison. And it's time to stop letting it hold you hostage.

Ask yourself this: if you met him today, knowing what you know now, would you still choose him? If the answer is no, then it's time to choose yourself.

The Courage To Let Go
Letting go isn't failure. It's bravery. It's saying, "I love myself enough to stop accepting less than I deserve." It's choosing yourself over the fear of the unknown. And when you do, you create space for something better. Something real. Something that doesn't require mental gymnastics to make you feel valued.

Here's My Five Steps To Letting Go:
1. **Acknowledge Your Worth:** Write down all the things that make you incredible. Remind yourself why you deserve better.

2. **Lean On Your Support System:** Call your friends, your family, your therapist. Surround yourself with people who love you.

3. **Set Boundaries:** Block his number if you need to. Unfollow him on social media. Create distance to protect your healing.

4. **Focus On Self-Care:** Reclaim your routines. Dive into the things you love. Journal, take long baths, read books that inspire you.

5. **Take It Day By Day:** Healing isn't linear. Some days will be harder than others. But every step forward is a step toward freedom.

Use the space below to write down all the things that make you incredible and why you deserve better.

_____

_____

_____

_____

_____

_____

_____

_____

_____

_____

_____

_____

_____

_____

_____

_____

_____

_____

The Other Side Of The Shift

What's waiting for you on the other side of the shift? Peace. Self-discovery. A love that doesn't feel like work. When you let go of what's breaking you, you make room for what can heal you.

When I faced my own shift, I was terrified. I cried, I doubted myself, I questioned everything. But as time passed, I realized that walking away was the most loving thing I'd ever done for myself. I found joy in my own company. I rediscovered my passions. And when love found me again, it was a love that didn't just fill the cracks—it built a new, stronger foundation.

The shift doesn't have to be the end. It can be the beginning. The beginning of asking yourself the questions that matter. Am I happy? Am I fulfilled? Is this the love I deserve?

Comfort vs. Complacency

We convince ourselves it's love when it feels comfortable. But comfort, my dear, is a double-edged sword. It's warm, familiar, and safe—until it's not. Until that comfort becomes the very thing suffocating you, keeping you from stepping into the life you're meant to have. And if you're anything like me, you've probably found yourself caught in that hazy in-between: questioning whether it's truly love or just the absence of loneliness. Let's unpack this together.

Comfort is the late-night takeout orders, the familiarity of his laugh, and the ease of not having to explain why you need two extra pillows on the bed. It's the way he knows exactly how you like your coffee—or, in my case, your white chocolate hot cocoa. It feels good, doesn't it? But here's the kicker: comfort can also be the way you've grown accustomed to his forgetfulness, the way you've learned to anticipate disappointment when he promises to show up and doesn't. Comfort can become the silence after a fight where you both retreat instead of repairing. It can be the subtle erosion of your self-worth, disguised as "I'm just keeping the peace."

Let's be real. How many times have we justified the late-night text that doesn't come? How many weekends have we spent forgiving thoughtless actions, clinging to the idea that "at least he's trying"? I've been there, and if I'm honest, I've stayed too long, more than once. Because when you're invested, walking away feels like giving up, like admitting you've wasted your time. But staying? That's a waste of your future.

Here's the hard truth: if someone is comfortable with seeing you hurt, they don't deserve the privilege of loving you. If they're comfortable watching you cry, apologizing only to repeat the same behavior, they're not your partner—they're your lesson. And trust me, lessons are important, but they're not meant to be lifelong companions.

The Late-Night Arguments

Let's talk about those late-night arguments. The ones where you find yourself raising your voice, trying to explain the same thing for the hundredth time, and still walking away unheard. The ones where he makes you feel like you're too much when, in reality, he's offering far too little. That's not love—it's complacency masquerading as effort.

I remember one argument in particular. I was explaining, for what felt like the thousandth time, how I needed more consistency. He sat there, nodding absently, and then hit me with, "You're overreacting." Overreacting? Because I'd like to feel prioritized in a relationship? My love, that's gaslighting 101.

It's in those moments you have to ask yourself: Am I fighting to be understood, or am I fighting to be respected? Because respect doesn't need to be fought for. Respect listens, leans in, and learns. And if you find yourself constantly justifying why your feelings matter, it's time to reassess.

Signs Someone's Too Comfortable Hurting You

So, how do you know when someone's too comfortable hurting you? It's in the way they respond when you're upset. Do they minimize your feelings, or do they lean in, genuinely wanting to make it better? Do they blame you for being "too sensitive," or do they take accountability? A King understands that his Queen's happiness isn't just her responsibility—it's theirs.

Here are a few red flags to watch for:

1. **Dismissiveness:** Do they brush off your concerns with, "It's not that big of a deal"?

2. **Repetitive Apologies:** Do they say sorry but change nothing?

3. **Defensiveness:** Do they turn the blame on you, making you feel like you're the problem?

4. **Emotional Neglect:** Do they check out emotionally, leaving you to carry the weight of the relationship alone?

The hard part is that these behaviors often start small. A forgotten date here, a dismissive comment there. But over time, they pile up until you're buried under the weight of unspoken resentment and unmet needs.

Action Steps To Break Free

So, what do you do when you realize you're stuck in a cycle of comfort and complacency? Here's the roadmap:

1. **Name It:** The first step is acknowledging what's happening. What are the recurring issues? How did they make you feel? Naming the problem gives you power over it.

2. **Visualize Your Ideal Relationship:** Close your eyes and imagine what love looks like for you. Is it someone who remembers your favorite flowers just because? Someone who holds space for your emotions without judgment? Use that vision as your guidepost.

_____

_____

_____

_____

_____

_____

_____

Write down the recurring issues and how they made you feel. Give the issue a name and speak to the name directly.

_____
_____
_____
_____
_____
_____
_____
_____
_____
_____
_____
_____
_____
_____
_____
_____
_____
_____
_____
_____
_____
_____
_____
_____
_____
_____

Now write down what love looks like to you.

_____

_____

_____

_____

_____

_____

_____

_____

_____

_____

_____

_____

_____

_____

_____

_____

_____

_____

_____

_____

_____

_____

_____

The Emotional Rollercoaster

Walking away from comfort feels like ripping off a band-aid—but instead of a quick sting, it's a slow, aching burn. You'll doubt yourself. You'll replay every memory, wondering if you overreacted or expected too much. Let me tell you this: wanting to feel loved, respected, and cherished is not asking too much. It's the bare minimum.

You might miss the good parts—the inside jokes, the lazy Sundays, the way he made you laugh until your sides hurt. But don't forget the tears, the loneliness you felt while sitting right next to him, the way you shrank yourself to keep the peace. Missing someone doesn't mean you made the wrong choice. It means you're human.

What's Waiting On The Other Side

When it comes to leaving comfort behind: it makes room for something extraordinary. The right partner won't just feel comfortable—they'll feel like home. They'll celebrate your highs, hold you through your lows, and never make you question your worth.

When I finally walked away from my "comfort," I found myself again. I rediscovered my passions, reconnected with friends I'd neglected, and built a life that felt full—even without a partner. And when love found me again, it was unlike anything I'd ever known. It was kind, intentional, and steady. It was a love that didn't just fit into my life—it elevated it.

Comfort is seductive, but it's not the same as love. Love challenges you to grow. It pushes you to be better while accepting you as you are. It's not flawless, but it's respectful, reciprocal, and real.

So, my dear friend, if you were sitting in a relationship that feels more like a security blanket than a partnership, it's time to ask yourself: Was I holding on because it's love, or because it's familiar? And if the answer is the latter, take a deep breath, pack up your emotional baggage, and continue to walk away. You deserve more than comfort—you deserve magic.

The Cost Of Waiting

Darling, let's talk—just you and me. Waiting is a thief. Not the kind that kicks down your door and takes your purse. No, this one is stealthier, subtler. She sneaks in and slowly steals your time, your joy, your energy, and worst of all, your sense of self. We've all had those moments where we're staring at our phones, willing it to light up, wondering if one more minute, one more hour, or one more day will change everything. Spoiler: it doesn't.

Waiting isn't sexy or empowering—it's exhausting. It's the emotional equivalent of wearing heels two sizes too small: it hurts, it's uncomfortable, and it's completely unnecessary. Yet we do it. We tell ourselves stories to make the waiting make sense. "He's just stressed." "It's a rough patch." "Things will get better." And so we stand on the corner of "what I deserve" and "what I'm settling for," hoping that some divine intervention will take us in the right direction.

But waiting doesn't work that way. It's not a magic spell or a guarantee that things will improve. Instead, it holds you hostage, keeping you tied to something—or someone—that may not even deserve you. Think about what all this waiting has cost you—not just in hours and days but in your peace of mind, your confidence, and all those beautiful opportunities you've let slip by. Every single day you wait is another day you're not fully living. It's another day you're not chasing your dreams, your happiness, or your potential. Waiting is this vicious cycle, spinning you between hope and disappointment, draining every ounce of strength you have left.

What Waiting Feels Like

Let's be real: waiting isn't just inconvenient; it's a slow burn that leaves you emotionally scorched. It's waking up and already knowing that nothing is going to change today. It's sitting across from someone at dinner who's more interested in their phone than your stories. It's lying awake at night, replaying every conversation, trying to decode words and actions like they're hieroglyphics. Waiting is like heartbreak on a loop—the pain keeps playing, and you don't know how to turn it off.

Waiting doesn't just drain you; it rewires you. It changes how you think about love, about yourself, and about what you deserve. It convinces you that crumbs are a feast and that silence is a sign of affection. Waiting makes you a master of making excuses, not just for them but for yourself. And honestly, darling, don't you deserve better than that?

And let's rip off the bandage to the truth: waiting isn't based on your patience. It's driven by fear. Fear of admitting that you deserve more. Fear of losing something you've already invested so much in. But here's the thing—waiting doesn't just waste your time. It distorts your reality. You're so busy hoping for what could be that you forget to see what is.

The Lies Waiting Tells You

The thing about waiting: it's sneaky. It dresses itself up in hope and tells you lies that sound almost convincing. Lies like:

- **"They'll Change If I'm patient enough."** Honey, change only happens when someone wants it. Your patience won't create their transformation.

- **"I'll Regret Leaving."** You're far more likely to regret staying in a situation that drains you.

- **"No One Else Will Love Me."** That's fear talking, not truth. Love exists—real, fulfilling love—and it's not limited to what you've already known.

- **"At Least I Know What To Expect."** Familiarity can feel safer than starting over, but let's be real— comfort isn't the same as happiness.

These lies create a false sense of security, convincing you that waiting is easier than stepping into the unknown. But let's not sugarcoat it: waiting isn't easy. It's exhausting. It chips away at your sense of self and robs you of the joy you deserve.

Knowing vs. Doing

When you choose to wait you are acknowledging that deep down, you already know. You know when the words don't match the actions. You know when their promises feel more like placeholders. You know when the love you're holding onto is just a shadow of what it used to be. But knowing and doing? Those are two different beasts.

You know he doesn't prioritize you. You know you've had the same argument so many times you could recite both parts like a script. You know you're holding on to the idea of who he was, not the reality of who he is now. But leaving? Walking away? That feels like tearing out a piece of your own heart. Yet, isn't it better to feel that sharp pain once than to endure the dull ache of waiting forever?

It's like trying to keep a plant alive in the dark. You keep watering it, hoping it'll grow, but it's never going to thrive without sunlight. And you, my dear, need sunlight. You need warmth and care and light, not endless nights of hoping for something that's no longer there.

Recognizing The Thief

So how do you know when waiting has become a thief in your life? Let me break it down for you:

1. **Constant Disappointment:** You're on a first-name basis with unmet expectations and broken promises.

2. **Emotional Drain:** The relationship leaves you feeling empty instead of fulfilled.

3. **Loss of Confidence:** You're starting to question your worth because your needs are constantly overlooked.

4. **Stagnation:** Your personal growth has hit a standstill because all your energy is spent hoping for change.

5. **Unrelenting Hope:** You're clinging to a fantasy of what could be, ignoring the reality of what is.

The scariest part? The longer you wait, the harder it becomes to move on. I have to bring this up just in case you are thinking about trying to find a way to go back. It's like quicksand—the more you struggle to justify staying, the deeper you sink.

Things You Might Recognize

If this is hitting close to home, you're not alone. Let's look at some of the red flags you've probably waved off:

1. **Making Excuses:** You've said it: "He's just going through something," "It's a phase," or "This is just how relationships are." But is it?

2. **Feeling Stuck:** You were in a holding pattern, waiting for him to notice you again, to love you the way you deserve. And the silence between those moments? It's deafening.

3. **The Loneliness:** Nothing is lonelier than being next to someone who makes you feel invisible. It's a constant reminder of what's missing.

4. **Losing Yourself:** You've looked in the mirror and thought, "Who am I? When did I become the girl who waits?" And that's a heartbreak all its own.

5. **Giving Too Much:** You keep giving—your time, your energy, your love—because you think it'll fix things. But what are you getting in return?

The Truth About Waiting

Here's the raw, unfiltered truth: waiting feels like you're doing something, but really, you're just stuck. It tricks you into thinking you're being hopeful or loyal, but what you're really doing is giving away the reins to your life. Love isn't a solo project, and it certainly shouldn't feel like a full-time job with no benefits.

Waiting convinces you that staying (or going back) is easier than leaving, that hope is better than action, that patience is the answer. But patience in the wrong situation? It's not a virtue—it's a slow death. Waiting for someone to see your worth isn't romantic—it's tragic. And you? You're not a tragedy. You're a masterpie still in progress.

This Is The Loudest I Can Tell It To You, Darling.

STOP WAITING!

YOU WAIT FOR NO ONE!

The IT Girl's Perspective On Rejection: Why It's A Redirection To Something Better

Rejection. It's the heartbreak no one wants to talk about, the gut-punch we pretend doesn't sting as much as it does. It pokes at the places we'd rather keep hidden: insecurities, old wounds, the question of whether we've somehow asked for too much. It's a thief of confidence in the moment it strikes, whispering lies about your worth and your place in the world. Truth be told, the IT Girl knows: rejection isn't a measure of worth. It's a matter of alignment. It's not the world telling you you're "not enough." It's the universe whispering, *this isn't your door—keep going.*

The IT Girl doesn't let rejection define her. She sees it for what it truly is: divine redirection—a blessing cloaked in the discomfort of being told "no." She understands that rejection isn't a sign of being unworthy; it's a reflection of being too much for the wrong fit. And being too much? That's a badge of honor. Why? Because it means you're making room for something—or someone—who is ready to match your energy. Someone who will see your fullness and celebrate it instead of being intimidated by it.

Rejection doesn't ask you to shrink; it challenges you to reflect. It asks you to stand still for a moment, uncomfortable as it may be, and reevaluate what you're chasing. Are you fighting for a door that won't open? Are you clinging to the hope that if you just tried harder, bent a little further, or dimmed your light a little more, you'd finally fit into someone else's world? The IT Girl knows better. She knows that when the door doesn't open, it's not a sign to change herself—it's a sign to change direction.

This isn't just about tolerating rejection; it's the audacity to celebrate it. It's the realization that being released from spaces that couldn't contain you is a gift. It's not easy—it's rarely easy—but it's worth it. Because every rejection clears the path for something greater, something that doesn't demand you compromise your identity just to feel accepted. It's the ultimate lesson in self-worth—the understanding that your "too much" is exactly what someone else is waiting for.

Rejection Isn't The End; It's The Beginning

Let's start with the sting. When rejection hits, it hurts. Whether it's a person, a job, or a dream, the feeling of being turned away feels like a cold slap. Your mind goes into overdrive, analyzing every moment, wondering if you could've said something different, been someone different, done more, been less. But pause. Take a breath. The initial sting is just that—a fleeting moment. It doesn't define you, and it doesn't dictate what's next.

Rejection is redirection. It's the universe stepping in and saying, *Not here. Not this.* It's your higher self protecting you from what isn't aligned with your worth, even when you can't see it yet. Think of the times rejection hurt most. Maybe it was a partner who didn't prioritize you or a job that overlooked your brilliance. At the time, it felt crushing. But now, with hindsight, don't you see how those closed doors led you to better ones? Each rejection, though painful, was a push toward something greater, even if it felt like a shove at the time.

Rejection forces you to confront what isn't working. It holds up a mirror to the situations where you were settling, whether you realized it or not. And that mirror? It's not your enemy. It's your guide.

The Liberation Of Letting Go

Let's talk about the art of letting go, not just as a necessary act, but as a radical reclamation of your power. Releasing what no longer serves you isn't just a process of moving on—it's a return to the full brightness of who you are. Imagine this: you've been bending, shrinking, and dimming your light to fit into someone else's world—a world so narrow it couldn't possibly contain the fullness of you. You tell yourself they'll change, that if you just love them harder, they'll finally see your worth. And when they don't, you make excuses for them, carrying the emotional weight of a relationship that feels like dragging a suitcase with a broken wheel.

Then comes the moment of rejection—the sharp sting of being let go. It feels like your heart has been cracked open, and for a moment, the pain is all you can see. But here's where the magic happens: in the aftermath of heartbreak, you realize that the weight you were carrying wasn't love—it was compromise. And suddenly, you're free. Free to stop begging for someone's time, attention, or validation. Free to find someone who values you without hesitation. Someone who shows up, not because you asked, but because they *want* to.

Rejection removes you from spaces that couldn't hold your brilliance. It isn't a loss—it's the creation of space for what's meant to find you. Letting go isn't just an act of release—it's an act of courage. It's looking at what hurt you and saying, *You don't control me anymore.* It's acknowledging the pain without letting it define you. And that's the IT Girl's secret:

she doesn't hold on to what weighs her down. She doesn't negotiate with heartbreak. She turns it into fuel.

Here's the one thing no one tells you about letting go: it's not about forgetting the person or the experience. It's about reframing it. Start by sitting with the memories that still sting. Allow yourself to feel them fully—the good, the bad, the beautiful, the ugly. And then ask yourself this: *What was I holding on to? Was it the person, or was it the hope of who I thought they could be?* Often, what we cling to isn't the reality of the relationship, but the potential we believed it had.

Now comes the secret tip, the one you won't hear anywhere else: write a goodbye letter, but don't send it. This isn't for them; it's for you. Pour everything into it. Write down what you loved, what hurt you, what you learned, and what you're letting go of. Then, at the end of the letter, write this sentence: *I release you, and in doing so, I release myself.* Keep the letter if you want a reminder of how far you've come, or destroy it as a ritual of closure. Either way, this act of writing will untangle the emotional knots that have been keeping you tied to the past.

Letting go is liberation disguised as heartbreak. It's the emotional equivalent of clearing out a closet overflowing with things that no longer fit. Painful in the moment, yes, but freeing when you see how much space you've created for something new. And let me tell you, darling, the IT Girl always makes room for better. Because she knows this: the lightness you feel when you finally let go isn't just relief—it's power. It's the weight of self-respect settling back where it belongs—right in your hands.

Take this time to write your goodbye letter.

_____

_____

_____

_____

_____

_____

_____

_____

_____

_____

_____

_____

_____

_____

_____

_____

_____

_____

_____

_____

_____

_____

_____

The IT Girl's Strategy For Navigating Rejection

An IT Girl doesn't let rejection derail her. She feels it—because she's human, after all—but she doesn't live there. She uses rejection as a mirror, a tool to reflect on what she truly wants and what she'll no longer tolerate.

1. **Reframe The Narrative**: Instead of spiraling into thoughts of *Why wasn't I enough?* she asks, *What wasn't right here?* The rejection becomes less about her and more about the misalignment. This is not based on blame; it's a matter of clarity. She understands that not everything is meant to be a match, and that's okay. Not everyone can meet her at her level.

2. **Feel It, Then Move**: The IT Girl doesn't pretend she's made of steel. She lets herself cry, vent, feel the sting. But she doesn't unpack her bags and live in the pain. Once the emotion is honored, she refocuses on the bigger picture: her growth, her goals, her worth. She knows that feelings are meant to be felt, not permanent addresses.

3. **Celebrate The Redirection**: She doesn't see rejection as a closed door; she sees it as a sign pointing her toward something greater. The rejection wasn't about failure; it was about protection. She celebrates the opportunity to realign, understanding that every rejection is a course correction.

A Realigned Path

Let's talk about the aftermath. After the tears have dried and the dust has settled, what comes next? The IT Girl steps back into her power. She understands that rejection isn't just about what's removed from her life—it's the opening for what's meant to take its place. She leans into her resilience, knowing that every "no" is one step closer to the resounding "yes" that's meant for her.

She also learns. Every rejection offers a lesson, a chance to refine what she wants and needs. That partner who couldn't show up? He taught her the importance of consistency. That job that overlooked her? It reminded her to never dull her brilliance for spaces that don't appreciate it. Every rejection becomes a stepping stone, a piece of the puzzle that leads to alignment.

Rejection also offers clarity. It strips away the illusions we cling to and forces us to see situations for what they are. It's not easy, but it's necessary. And once the clarity sets in, the IT Girl doesn't just move on—she moves forward, stronger and more aligned than ever.

What Rejection Really Teaches Us

Here's the profound truth: rejection isn't the end; it's a beginning. It's a reset button, a chance to start fresh with more clarity and strength than before. It's not about the person or opportunity that said no. It's the life that's saying yes to you. And the IT Girl? She leans into that yes with her whole heart.

Rejection teaches resilience. It reminds you that your worth isn't tied to someone else's acceptance. It shows you that the closed door wasn't a loss—it was protection from what wasn't meant for you. And with every rejection, you grow.

You learn to let go of what no longer serves you and to make room for what does.

So, the next time rejection comes knocking, don't see it as a loss. See it as a redirection. See it as the God stepping in and saying, *This isn't for you, but something better is.* And remember, every rejection is proof that you're not for everyone—and that's exactly how it should be.

Darling, you don't need everyone to choose you. You just need the right ones to show up. And they will, when the time is right.

The Fear Of Letting Go

Let's cut to the chase: leaving is terrifying. It's stepping off that train platform into the unknown, and the unknown can be downright scary. It means confronting loneliness, starting over, and admitting that you might have been wrong. But staying? Staying in a relationship that's not working? That's its own kind of loneliness. It's waking up every day feeling unseen, unheard, and unvalued.

Here's what I want you to hear, loud and clear: leaving does not epitomize failure. It's an act of self-honor. It's the realization that your time, energy, and happiness are too precious to waste on waiting for someone else to see your worth.

And yes, the unknown is full of "what-ifs." What if I never find love again? What if I'm making a mistake? What if I regret leaving? But, my love, the unknown also holds promise: What if you rediscover your passions? What if you build a life that feels whole? What if you find a love that doesn't require waiting?

Choosing Yourself

Leaving the station doesn't mean you've failed—it means you've finally chosen you. It means deciding that your time, your energy, your life are worth more than the empty promises of a delayed train. It means understanding that the cost of waiting is too high and the reward of letting go is priceless.

Here's how you take those first steps:

1. **Face The Reality:** Be brutally honest with yourself. Write down how waiting has impacted your life—the good, the bad, and the heartbreaking.

2. **Seek Perspective:** Talk it out with someone you trust. Sometimes your best friend's outside perspective is exactly what you need to see things clearly.

3. **Give Yourself Grace:** Letting go is a process, not a single moment. Be kind to yourself as you navigate this new chapter.

How has waiting impacted your life? What do you feel that you were waiting for?

_____

_____

_____

_____

_____

_____

_____

_____

_____

_____

_____

_____

_____

_____

_____

_____

_____

_____

_____

_____

_____

_____

The Other Side Of Waiting

So, what happens when you finally stop waiting? Freedom. Growth. Possibility. When you let go of what's holding you back, you create space for something better—a love that doesn't make you question your worth, a life that feels full and vibrant, a version of yourself you haven't seen in years.

Imagine waking up and feeling light instead of heavy. Imagine chasing your dreams without the weight of someone else's indifference holding you back. Imagine a love that feels like partnership instead of patience. Imagine a life where your joy doesn't depend on someone else's approval.

When I finally let go of my own waiting game, it was like jumping into cold water. It shocked me, disoriented me, but ultimately, it refreshed me. I found myself again. I reconnected with my passions, rebuilt my confidence, and discovered joy in my own company. And when love found me again, it was steady, kind, and real—not something I had to wait for, but something I was finally ready to receive.

Breaking The Cycle

If you're trapped in the waiting game, here's how to break free:

1. **Call Out the Lies:** Write down the thoughts that keep you waiting and challenge them. Are they fear-based or factual?

2. **Picture Your Future:** Close your eyes and imagine your life without waiting. What does it look like? How does it feel? Let that vision guide you.

3. **Take Baby Steps:** You don't need to leap overnight. Start small—reclaim your time, your hobbies, and your energy.

4. **Celebrate Yourself:** Every step you take is a victory. Recognize your courage and resilience.

5. **Embrace the Unknown:** Shift your perspective. The unknown isn't something to fear—it's something to explore.

Here is your space to write it out.

_____

_____

_____

_____

_____

_____

_____

_____

_____

_____

_____

_____

_____

_____

The Benefits Of Letting Go

Letting go isn't easy—it's one of the hardest things you'll ever do. But it's also one of the most liberating. When you let go of what's not meant for you, you create space for what is. You free yourself from the weight of unfulfilled expectations, from the pain of holding on to something that hurts more than it heals.

The benefits of letting go are profound:

- **Freedom:** Letting go gives you the freedom to focus on yourself, your happiness, and your growth.

- **Clarity:** It allows you to see the relationship for what it was, not what you wished it could be.

- **Self-Worth:** It's a declaration that you deserve better, that you're no longer willing to settle for less.

- **New Beginnings:** Letting go opens the door to new opportunities, new experiences, and new love.

Letting go isn't the end—it's a beginning. It's a chance to start over, to rewrite your story, to create a life that's aligned with your worth and your desires. It's a powerful act of self-love, and it's a gift you give to yourself. Because at the end of the day, you are your own happily ever after.

When you stop waiting, you start living. You take back your time, your energy, and your joy. Imagine waking up and feeling light instead of heavy. Imagine chasing dreams without someone else's indifference holding you back. Imagine being in a relationship where love feels mutual, not like a puzzle you're constantly trying to solve.

When I finally stopped waiting, it felt like jumping into cold water. It shocked me, disoriented me, but ultimately, it refreshed me. I found myself again. I reconnected with my passions, my friends, and my own company. And when love found me again, it wasn't something I had to wait for. It was steady, kind, and real.

Stopping waiting doesn't just change your relationship status; it changes your life. It's reclaiming your power, your freedom, and your sense of self. You're stepping into a life where you're no longer defined by someone else's decisions or lack of action.

Does The How Really Matter?

Let's face it: we're all guilty of obsessing over the how. How did he change? How did we go from sharing late-night dreams to choking on strained silence over dinner? How did he stop being the man who made us feel invincible and start being the man who makes us question our worth?

The how feels important, doesn't it? It gives us a sense of control, a belief that if we can pinpoint the moment everything fell apart, we can somehow piece it back together. But here's the hard truth: the how doesn't matter as much as we think it does. Knowing why someone hurt you doesn't make the hurt go away. Understanding how a glass shattered doesn't make it unbreakable again.

And yet, we can't help ourselves. We replay every conversation, dissect every argument, and analyze every decision. We pore over his words, looking for hidden meanings. We scan his actions, searching for signs. Was it me? Was it something I did? Could I have stopped this? It's like trying to solve a mystery when the clues are deliberately vague. But the problem with chasing the how is that it keeps us tethered to the past, clinging to a version of the relationship that's already crumbled.

The Dangerous Comfort Of The How

This is what happens about obsessing over the how: it becomes deceptively comforting. It feels like action. It feels like progress. But really, it's a distraction—a way to avoid the truth staring us in the face. The truth that no matter the why or the how, the outcome remains the same. He's wasn't showing up for you. The version of him you're mourning isn't the version standing in front of you. And no amount of analyzing is going to bring him back.

Think about it. Does knowing the why change anything? If you knew exactly what made him stop trying, would it have erased the late-night tears? Would it have made the dinners filled with silence any less painful? Would it have turn his indifference into affection? Or is the how just a way to avoid asking yourself the harder question: what now?

The Never-Ending Loop Of Blame

Obsessing over the how keeps us trapped in a cycle of self-blame and what-ifs. We think, "If I had done this differently, maybe he'd still be here." "If I had just been more patient, more understanding, more perfect, maybe we'd still be happy." But here's the kicker: relationships aren't math equations. They don't fail because of one misstep or one missed opportunity. They fail because two people stopped moving in the same direction.

The danger in blaming yourself is that it blinds you to the bigger picture. It keeps you focused on fixing something that might not be fixable. It's like trying to rebuild a house with a foundation that's already cracked. You can keep adding bricks, but eventually, it's all going to collapse.

What The How Can't Do

The how is seductive because it promises clarity. It whispers that if we can just figure out the reason, we can make it all better. Let's be clear: even if you get the answer, it's rarely satisfying. It's rarely the neat, tidy explanation you want it to be. And even if it is, what then? Do you forgive him? Do you forget? Do you move on together? Or do you finally admit that knowing the why doesn't change the fact that the relationship was no longer serving you?

Instead of chasing the how, ask yourself this: how does he make me feel every day? How did this relationship support my happiness, my growth, my self-worth? Because those questions? They matter more than the how ever will.

The Reality Check

Here's a reality check: people change. Circumstances change. And sometimes, relationships change in ways we can't control. It doesn't mean you failed. It doesn't mean you weren't enough. It means that the version of love you had no longer fits the version of life you're living now.

The how keeps you stuck. It keeps you looking backward when what you need is to move forward. Instead of focusing on what went wrong, focus on what's happening now. The why doesn't matter. What matters is deciding what comes next.

What's Next?

The real question isn't how he changed. It's what you're going to do about it. Are you going to keep clinging to the hope that he'll magically turn back into the man you fell in love with and come back for you? Or are you going to accept that the relationship you were fighting for might not be the one you deserve?

The truth about moving forward: it's terrifying. Letting go of the how means letting go of the illusion of control. It means admitting that some things are beyond your power to fix. But it also means freedom. Freedom to stop replaying the past. Freedom to stop dissecting every word and every action. Freedom to start focusing on yourself.

How To Let Go Of The How

Talk To Your Thoughts. Tell Your Thoughts, Thanks For Stopping By But That Was The Past. You Are Done Crying And Thinking About It. Simply Say That's An Interesting Thought But Here Is One Better - Counteract It With A Better Thought Or Just Stop And Say 'That Is An Interesting Thought.'

Here is your space to write out your thoughts.

_____

_____

_____

_____

_____

_____

_____

_____

_____

_____

_____

_____

_____

_____

_____

_____

_____

_____

_____

_____

_____

_____

_____

_____

_____

The Truth About Moving Forward

Moving forward doesn't mean forgetting. It doesn't mean pretending the relationship didn't matter. It means recognizing that holding on to the past isn't helping you build the future. It means valuing yourself enough to walk away from what no longer serves you.

When I finally let go of chasing the how, it felt like a weight had been lifted. The questions stopped swirling in my mind. The blame stopped eating away at me. And for the first time in a long time, I could see a future that didn't include trying to fix something that wasn't mine to fix.

Letting go doesn't mean you stop caring; it means you start caring for yourself more. It's an act of self-preservation and self-love—a way to reclaim your power and your peace. And when you do, you create space for something new, something better, something worthy of the incredible person you are.

The how is seductive, but it's a trap. It keeps you stuck in a cycle of analysis and self-blame. It keeps you tethered to a version of the relationship that no longer exists. The truth is, the how doesn't matter as much as the what now. So stop chasing answers that won't change the outcome. Stop holding on to someone who isn't holding on to you.

Choose yourself. Choose happiness. Choose to move forward. Because the only thing worse than being hurt is staying hurt. And the only thing worse than losing someone who doesn't value you is losing yourself in the process.

So, my love, let go of the how. Walk into your future with your head high and your heart open. Because the best things in life don't need dissecting—they just need living.

The Turning Point

There's always a moment. A moment when the weight of the excuses becomes too heavy to carry. Maybe it's something small, like seeing him online but not responding to your message. Or maybe it's something big, like realizing he's making time for everyone but you. Whatever it is, it hits you like a ton of bricks: this isn't love. This is complacency disguised as companionship.

And in that moment, you have a choice. You can keep waiting, hoping he'll wake up and realize what he's about to lose. Or you can wake up and realize you deserve more than this. You deserve someone who doesn't make you question your worth. Someone who shows up without you having to beg. Someone who loves you the way you've always dreamed of being loved.

The Chase: Why Are You Running After Love?

Let's get one thing straight—a Queen, The IT Girl you are doesn't chase. She doesn't beg for attention or affection or respect. She doesn't lower her standards to fit into someone else's world. She doesn't wait for someone to choose her. She chooses herself.

So why are you chasing? Why are you running after someone who isn't running after you? Why are you putting all your energy into a relationship that isn't putting anything back into you? Why are you settling for breadcrumbs when you deserve the whole feast?

The real truth about chasing—it's exhausting. It drains you emotionally, mentally, and physically. It makes you feel like you're not enough, like you have to prove your worth to someone who should already see it. And the worst part? It rarely leads to anything good. Because if someone isn't choosing you willingly, no amount of chasing will change that.

What Do You See For Yourself?

Take a moment and ask yourself this: What do you see for your future? Is it this? Is it a lifetime of waiting for him to call, wondering if he cares, feeling like an afterthought? Is it shrinking yourself to fit into his world, compromising your dreams to accommodate his indifference, sacrificing your happiness for the illusion of stability?

Or do you see something more? Do you see a love that feels like partnership, like mutual respect, like effort? Do you see someone who shows up for you, who values you, who makes you feel like a priority? Do you see a life where you wake up every day feeling cherished, supported, and loved?

Because that's what you deserve. And the only way to get it is to let go of what isn't serving you.

The Wake-Up Call

This is your wake-up call. The moment you stop settling for less. The moment you stop waiting for him to change. The moment you stop excusing his behavior and start holding him accountable. Because here's the thing—he's not going to change. Not unless he wants to. And if he hasn't already, what makes you think he ever will?

So, let this be the moment you choose yourself. The moment you decide that your happiness, your worth, your future matter more than the history you share with someone who doesn't see your value. Let this be the moment you stop living for potential and start living for reality.

Part 2:
Reclaiming Your Power

The IT Girl Confidence: Rising After Heartbreak

Let's talk about it, darling—the aftermath of a relationship ending. Whether it was a breakup that shattered your world, a divorce that redefined your future, or a situationship that left you questioning your worth, heartbreak has a way of shaking your very core. Confidence, once steady and luminous, can feel like it's slipping through your grasp. You start wondering if you were too much or not enough, and those whispers of self-doubt creep in, louder than ever.

But even the IT Girl—with her poise, her strength, her undeniable allure—isn't immune to those moments of uncertainty. What sets her apart isn't that she avoids the fall; it's how she rises after it. She doesn't let heartbreak define her—she lets it refine her. She doesn't cower in the shadows of what was; she steps boldly into the light of what could be. Confidence doesn't mean never stumbling; it's the unwavering belief in your ability to stand back up—stronger, wiser, and more radiant than before...

What Heartbreak Does To Your Confidence

When a relationship ends, it doesn't just take the love you shared—it can take pieces of your identity if you let it. Maybe you started to define yourself through their eyes, through their compliments, their attention, their approval. And when they're gone, it can feel like they've taken that version of you with them. Suddenly, you're standing in front of the mirror, not recognizing the person staring back at you.

Let me introduce you to Claire. Claire was the kind of woman who walked into boardrooms and commanded respect without saying a word. But then she met Ryan. Ryan was charming, funny, and endlessly supportive—until he wasn't. It started subtly: he would joke about how much time she spent on her career, how her ambition sometimes made her "intimidating." "You know, not every guy would be okay with how driven you are," he'd say with a smirk, as though his acceptance was a favor she should be grateful for.

At first, Claire brushed it off, thinking it was harmless. But over time, his words seeped into her psyche. She started hesitating before speaking up in meetings, questioning whether her boldness was too much. She stopped celebrating her wins with the same enthusiasm, afraid it might make Ryan feel smaller. One night, as they sat at dinner, she shared news about a promotion she had been working toward for months. Ryan barely looked up from his phone and muttered, "That's great, babe," before changing the subject to his own work drama.

When their relationship ended, Claire was left with an unsettling realization. It wasn't just the end of her relationship with Ryan—it was the end of the relationship she once had with herself. She wasn't mourning him; she was mourning the version of herself that had stopped showing up, piece by piece, to accommodate his insecurities.

This is where the hard questions come in: *Was I enough? Was it my fault? Did I miss the signs?* These questions, while painful, are also pivotal. Claire realized she had ignored her own intuition, dimmed her light to make someone else shine, and allowed her boundaries to blur.

Heartbreak has a sneaky way of making you question everything, especially yourself. It's not just the relationship that ends—it's often your trust in your own instincts, your ability to make good decisions, and your sense of self-worth that takes a hit. You start second-guessing the moments where you could have spoken up but stayed silent, the times you ignored your gut because love told you to stay. Doubt manifests in subtle ways—hesitating before making decisions, replaying conversations in your head, or overanalyzing every interaction. It can feel like you're walking through quicksand, unsure if your footing is strong enough to hold you.

But rebuilding confidence begins with small yet profound actions. First, you have to stop seeing yourself through the lens of your heartbreak. Instead of asking, "Why didn't I see this coming?" ask, "What can I learn from this?" Take those bruised moments and use them as stepping stones. Start trusting yourself again in everyday decisions—saying yes to opportunities that scare you a little, standing firm in your boundaries, or allowing yourself to walk away when something doesn't feel right. Confidence grows in the small wins, in the quiet moments where you choose yourself first.

Rebuilding Confidence After Heartbreak

Here's where the IT Girl shines. She knows that confidence isn't something handed to you by another person—it's something you cultivate, especially in the aftermath of loss. Rebuilding your confidence is about taking inventory of what was bruised and deciding to heal with intention.

1. **Own Your Part.** This is the hard one, but it's also the most transformative. Confidence begins with

accountability. Take a clear-eyed look at the relationship and ask yourself:

- o What did I ignore because I didn't want to face it?

- o Where did I settle for less than I deserved?

- o What patterns of mine allowed this dynamic to continue?

Owning your part is not centered on blaming yourself— it's the act of reclaiming your power. Because when you see where you went wrong, you also see where you can go right. Accountability isn't punishment; it's liberation.

2. **Forgive Yourself.** Maybe you stayed too long. Maybe you made excuses for them. Maybe you saw the red flags and chose to paint them green. Forgive yourself. You made those choices with the knowledge and emotional capacity you had at the time. Confidence is rooted in self-compassion. You can't rebuild if you're still tearing yourself down.

3. **Reconnect With Who You Are.** Heartbreak often makes you forget the amazing person you were before the relationship began. Reconnect with her. What did you love to do when you weren't bending to accommodate someone else? What made you feel alive, unstoppable, magnetic? Confidence is about returning to yourself, not recreating yourself.

4. **Set New Standards** The IT Girl knows that heartbreak is a lesson in boundaries and standards. Use this time to redefine what you will and will not accept in love. Confidence comes from knowing what you deserve and refusing to settle for anything less.

   Write it down: *I will never again stay in a situation where I feel unseen, unheard, or unvalued.* Make your standards non-negotiable.

So, let's answer some questions.

_____

_____

_____

_____

_____

_____

_____

_____

_____

_____

_____

_____

_____

_____

_____

_____

_____

What did I ignore because I did not want to face it? In what ways did I settle for less than what I deserved? What patterns of mine allowed the dynamic to continue?

_____

_____

_____

_____

_____

_____

_____

_____

_____

_____

_____

_____

_____

_____

_____

_____

_____

_____

_____

_____

_____

_____

What do I forgive myself for?

_____

_____

_____

_____

_____

_____

_____

_____

_____

_____

_____

_____

_____

_____

_____

_____

_____

_____

_____

_____

_____

_____

_____

_____

_____

_____

What did I love to do when I wasn't bending to accommodate someone else? What made me feel alive, unstoppable and magnetic?

_____

_____

_____

_____

_____

_____

_____

_____

_____

_____

_____

_____

_____

_____

_____

_____

_____

_____

_____

_____

_____

_____

_____

_____

Write this down until you mean it.

I will never again stay in a situation where I feel unseen, unheard, or unvalued.

_____

_____

_____

_____

_____

_____

_____

_____

_____

_____

_____

_____

_____

_____

_____

_____

_____

_____

_____

_____

_____

The Importance Of Confidence In Love

Confidence is the foundation of every decision you make, every boundary you set, and every relationship you allow into your life. It's the inner force that keeps you from shrinking when someone subtly undermines your value. It's the resolve that helps you stand tall and walk away from love that asks you to trade your authenticity for approval. And most importantly, it's the unspoken energy that draws the kind of love that celebrates your spirit instead of trying to reshape it.

When you're confident, fear stops steering the ship. You stop negotiating with yourself for scraps of love because you know your worth isn't up for debate. Instead of overexplaining why you deserve respect or over-apologizing for wanting to be heard, you hold your ground with quiet assurance. Confidence whispers: *You are enough, just as you are—without justification, without conditions.*

What A Confident Woman Does

The IT Girl moves through the world like she's carrying a secret only she knows. She's not flawless, but she's deeply rooted in who she is. Here's the unspoken magic behind her confidence:

- **She Makes Decisions With Intention:** A confident woman doesn't hesitate when her gut speaks. Take Olivia, for example. She was offered a promotion that would require moving to a new city, but her partner insisted it would "complicate things." For a moment, she wavered, but then she asked herself, "Will saying no honor who I am?" She accepted the offer. Her clarity wasn't about selfishness—it was about staying true to her values.

- **She Doesn't Seek Validation:** Confidence isn't built on universal approval; it flourishes in the presence of the right ones. Imagine Ava, who spent years overextending herself in friendships where she was always the giver. One day, she realized: "I don't need to prove my worth by doing more." She stepped back, and to her surprise, the real friends stayed—and stepped up.

- **She Prioritizes Her Well-Being:** Call it self-preservation or self-love; the IT Girl knows her energy is finite. Let's talk about Mia, who used to say yes to every social invite, even when she was exhausted. One Friday night, she stayed in, put on her favorite movie, and realized the world wouldn't fall apart if she chose herself. That's the IT Girl move: recharging unapologetically.

- **She Owns Her Voice:** Confidence means speaking your truth, even when it feels risky. Picture Lily during a family dinner, finally standing up to her relative who always made passive-aggressive remarks about her career. "I love what I do, and it works for me," she said calmly, meeting their eyes. Her voice didn't just set a boundary—it reclaimed her space. Silence isn't peace—it's the breeding ground for resentment. And clarity? That's her love language.

Love As Self-Discovery: The Healing After Heartbreak

Heartbreak often masquerades as the end, but the IT Girl sees through the disguise. It's not just the loss of a partner; it's the release of illusions, the breaking of unhealthy cycles, and the reclamation of the pieces of herself she once gave away too easily. If love had blurred the lines of her identity, heartbreak sharpens the focus—a painful yet necessary recalibration.

It's here, in the wreckage, that she uncovers the profound truth: heartbreak isn't just an event; it's a revelation. It's a chance to rewrite the narrative she'd been living—this time, with herself at the center, unashamedly whole and unapologetically real.

Why Heartbreak Transforms Her Into Her Truest Self:

1. **It Uncovers Her Blind Spots:** Heartbreak acts as a magnifying glass, showing her the places where she'd settled, ignored her needs, or tolerated less than she deserved. It's a reckoning with the habits and compromises she can no longer allow.

2. **It Reclaims Her Identity:** In the aftermath of a breakup, she's left with the question: Who am I without them? And the answer is as liberating as it is empowering—she's more than enough. She discovers that her identity was never tied to the relationship, but to her courage to stand on her own.

3. **It Builds Her Emotional Resilience:** Each tear shed and each sleepless night is a testament to her strength. Heartbreak doesn't destroy her—it fortifies her, making her capable of thriving in ways she never thought possible.

Here's the revelation: heartbreak doesn't leave her broken; it leaves her rebuilt. Every crack in her facade becomes a portal to her growth. And she doesn't just recover—she emerges, bold and unafraid, prepared for the love she now knows she truly deserves.

Moving Forward: The IT Girl's Promise To Herself

You've been through it all—the dizzying highs, the devastating heartbreaks, and the lessons etched into your soul. But let's get one thing straight: the ending of a relationship is not the ending of you. It's a redirection, a recalibration, and a reminder that your story is still being written.

Confidence after heartbreak doesn't just magically reappear—it's rebuilt, moment by moment, choice by choice. And as you step forward, you owe yourself a promise. Not a vague affirmation, but a set of non-negotiables rooted in the lessons you've learned. This promise has nothing to do with anyone else—it's a vow to yourself, a declaration of unwavering commitment to never abandon who you are again.

1. Trusting Your Intuition: Listening Without Doubt

Let's be real: how many times did your gut whisper something wasn't right, and you hushed it? Maybe it was that twinge when your partner's words didn't match their actions or the unease you felt when you were giving more than you were receiving. Ignoring your intuition isn't just self-betrayal; it's a disservice to your ability to protect your peace.

I Want To Tell You About Sophie. Sophie was in a relationship where everything looked ideal on paper. Her partner was attentive and charming, but something always felt slightly off—like there was an underlying disconnect she couldn't quite pinpoint off. When he started canceling plans last-minute or dodging deeper conversations, her gut told her to pay attention. But instead of trusting herself, she rationalized his behavior: "He's just depressed," she thought. It wasn't until she caught him lying that she realized her intuition had been right all along.

What To Do: Start small. Practice tuning into your gut during everyday decisions. When something feels off, ask yourself: *What is my body telling me?* Is it a tightness in your chest? A heaviness in your stomach? Trust these signals—they're there to guide you.

Unique Tip: Create a "gut check" ritual. When faced with uncertainty, step away from the noise—no texting friends for opinions, no overthinking. Instead, take five quiet minutes to sit with yourself. Ask: *What feels true for me right now?* Your intuition is like a muscle; the more you trust it, the stronger it becomes.

2. Valuing Your Peace: The Uncompromising Standard

Here's another hard truth: if it costs you your peace, it's too expensive. In relationships, we often make tiny trades—our time, our energy, our boundaries—in exchange for love or connection. But peace is the currency of a confident woman, and she guards it fiercely.

Let Me Tell You About Julia. Julia, was constantly on edge in her last relationship. Her partner's mood swings dictated the atmosphere of every evening. She'd tiptoe around his temper, apologizing for things she hadn't done, just to keep the peace. It wasn't until the relationship ended that Julia realized she hadn't known true peace in years. "I was surviving, not living," she confessed.

What To Do: Start protecting your peace like it's your most prized possession. Before committing to anything—a conversation, a relationship, a night out—ask yourself: *Will this add to my peace or subtract from it?*

Unique Tip: Create a "peace inventory." List the people, activities, and habits that bring you calm versus those that drain you. Slowly phase out the things on the draining list. Whether it's setting boundaries with a friend who constantly unloads their drama or unfollowing accounts that make you feel less than, this is not based on guilt—it's an act of self-preservation.

Let's Do This Now.

List the people, activities and habits that bring you peace and calm you.

_____

_____

_____

_____

_____

_____

_____

_____

_____

_____

3. Keeping Growth At The Forefront: Confidence As A Daily Choice

Confidence isn't static—it's alive, evolving, and deeply personal. It's not just a feeling; it's a practice, an ongoing conversation you have with yourself. The IT Girl doesn't just wake up confident; she makes deliberate choices that reinforce her self-worth every day.

Now Take Vanessa. Vanessa is now fresh out of a situationship that left her questioning everything. "Was I asking for too much? Was I even worthy of love?" she wondered. But instead of spiraling, Vanessa took a different approach. She started learning a new language, signed up for a dance class, and finally booked that solo trip she'd been dreaming of. Every step wasn't just about growth—it was a reclamation of her power.

What To Do: Start leaning into discomfort. Growth doesn't come from staying in your comfort zone—it comes from stepping outside of it. Take that class you've been eyeing. Apply for the job that intimidates you. Confidence isn't really about knowing you'll succeed—it's the certainty that you'll be okay, no matter the outcome.

Unique Tip: Create a "growth jar." Every time you do something outside your comfort zone, write it down and place it in the jar. On days when you're doubting yourself, read through those slips of paper. Let them remind you of your resilience and capacity to keep growing.

4. Owning Your Accountability: The Power of Self-Awareness

Let's not sugarcoat it: part of rebuilding confidence is taking a hard look in the mirror. It's asking yourself not just what went wrong, but what role you played in letting it continue. Accountability isn't centered on blame—it's a catalyst for empowerment.

Now I Call Her Very Relatable Tyra. Tyra stayed in a toxic relationship far longer than she should have. Her partner constantly invalidated her feelings, yet she stayed, hoping things would change. "I kept thinking, 'If I just love him harder, he'll get better,'" she admitted. When the relationship finally ended, she had to face a painful truth: she had ignored every red flag because she was afraid of being alone.

What To Do: Ask yourself the hard questions: *What did I allow? Where did I ignore my intuition?* Then, forgive yourself for those choices. Accountability has nothing to do with punishing yourself—it's a commitment to always stand by yourself.

Unique Tip: Write a "lessons learned" letter to yourself. List everything you've taken away from past relationships—not just what hurt, but what it taught you. End the letter with a promise: *I will never ignore my worth again.*

Take Some Time To Do This.

My Lessons Learned Letter

_____
_____
_____
_____
_____
_____
_____
_____
_____
_____
_____
_____
_____
_____
_____
_____
_____
_____
_____
_____
_____
_____
_____
_____

5. Moving Forward With Unapologetic Standards

The IT Girl doesn't lower her standards for convenience. She doesn't tolerate love that feels like a negotiation. Her standards aren't about being difficult—they're about being discerning.

Let Me Tell You About Emily. Emily met someone new, someone who seemed to check all the boxes. But when he started making jokes at her expense, she felt a familiar twinge of discomfort. Old Emily might have laughed it off, but the IT Girl in her said, "No, this doesn't work for me." She ended things before they could go further—not because she was afraid of being hurt, but because she refused to ignore her worth.

What To Do: Define your non-negotiables. These aren't just preferences—they're your values. Write them down, and revisit them every time you meet someone new. If they don't align, it's not a match, no matter how charming they seem.

Unique Tip: Practice saying "no" in low-stakes situations. Decline the party you don't want to attend or the favor you don't have time for. The more you reinforce your boundaries in everyday life, the easier it becomes to enforce them in love.

Right here, right now, define your non-negotiables.

_____

_____

_____

_____

_____

_____

_____

_____

_____

_____

_____

_____

_____

_____

_____

_____

_____

_____

_____

_____

_____

_____

_____

_____

_____

Confidence isn't wrapped in flawlessness—it's rooted in resilience. It's the unwavering trust that no matter what happens, you will always have your own back. So here's the promise, love: never again will you dim your light to make someone else shine. Never again will you trade your peace for the illusion of love. And never again will you question your worth—because you already know you're priceless. You don't just deserve a great love story; you deserve *your* love story, written on your own terms. And that? That's the ultimate IT Girl move.

The IT Girl Confidence: A Love Letter To Your Rebirth

Let's pause for a moment and reflect on this truth: no heartbreak, no failed relationship, no situation that left you questioning your worth has the power to extinguish your light. You, my love, are the IT Girl, and while heartbreak might have shaken you, it has also prepared you. You are not broken—you are evolving. And this chapter? It's the revival of your confidence, your voice, and your power.

Heartbreak doesn't just bruise your heart; it can bruise your identity. Suddenly, the woman who once knew what she brought to the table starts to wonder if she's enough. Doubts creep in, not just about love, but about herself. But let me remind you of something essential: confidence doesn't come from being loved by someone else. It comes from knowing, deep in your bones, that you are worthy of love simply because you exist.

What Heartbreak Taught You—And What It Didn't

Here's the first thing you need to know: heartbreak might have taught you about loss, but it didn't take away your ability to love, your brilliance, or your magic. It didn't erase the version of you who was bold and magnetic—it only made her harder to see for a little while. And now, it's time to call her back.

Let's get clear about what happened: maybe you stayed too long, ignored too much, or bent so far backward that you forgot what it felt like to stand tall. That's okay. We've all been there. Confidence isn't based on pretending you've always had it together—it's the decision to rebuild, even when you feel shattered. It's the courage to be honest with yourself, even when it stings: *I allowed someone to dim my light, but I won't let it happen again.*

Rebuilding Confidence: The Blueprint

Confidence isn't something you stumble into—it's something you cultivate. And rebuilding it after heartbreak means rewriting the stories you've been telling yourself.

Rewriting The Narrative

Confidence thrives in clarity. And clarity comes when you stop telling yourself the old, tired story of not being enough. Stop looking at the past as proof that you're unworthy, and start seeing it as evidence of your resilience.

Here's a new narrative: *I am a woman who loves deeply, who learns fiercely, and who never stops growing.* Every experience, even the painful ones, has been a step toward becoming the woman you're meant to be. Write that down. Read it until you believe it. And then act like it's true—because it is.

Now it is your turn to rewrite your narrative.

_____

_____

_____

_____

_____

_____

_____

_____

_____

_____

_____

_____

_____

_____

_____

_____

_____

_____

_____

_____

_____

_____

_____

_____

The IT Girl Promise: Never Again

Here's the part where you draw the line. Confidence is knowing what you will never again tolerate. So let's get specific.

- **Never again will you make yourself small to make someone else comfortable.**

- **Never again will you ignore your gut when it tells you something isn't right.**

- **Never again will you trade your peace for someone else's chaos.**

These aren't just promises—they're declarations. They're the foundation for the life and love you're building. Confidence has nothing to do with being without faults—it's the unshakable belief in your worth, even when the world tries to convince you otherwise.

Now, write out your Never Agains.

_____

_____

_____

_____

_____

_____

_____

_____

_____

_____

_____

_____

_____

_____

_____

_____

_____

_____

_____

_____

_____

_____

_____

When She Stood Tall Again

I have to tell you about Simone. Simone was in a relationship that started out like a dream and ended like a slow-burning fire. At first, everything was effortless. But as time went on, the cracks began to show. Her partner's words started to feel like backhanded compliments. "You're so independent; it's almost intimidating," he'd say with a smile that didn't quite reach his eyes. Slowly, Simone started questioning herself. Was she too much? Too bold? Too ambitious?

When the relationship ended, Simone was left with more questions than answers. But instead of wallowing, she decided to rebuild. She started small. She signed up for a boxing class she'd always wanted to try. She reconnected with old friends and said yes to a spontaneous weekend trip. Each little act was a way of reclaiming herself.

One day, she ran into her ex at a café. He looked surprised to see her—radiant, laughing, unapologetically herself. He fumbled through small talk, asking how she was. Simone smiled and said, "I'm thriving, actually." And the best part? She meant it.

What Confidence Looks Like In Action

Confidence isn't focused on loud declarations or carefully crafted social media posts. It's in the quiet, powerful ways you show up for yourself every day. Here's what the IT Girl does differently:

- **She Listens To Herself:** If something feels off, she doesn't dismiss it. Whether it's a red flag on a date or a job offer that doesn't align with her goals, she trusts her gut over anyone else's opinion.

- **She Chooses Her Peace:** Drama isn't her currency. If a situation, person, or opportunity disrupts her peace, she walks away without hesitation.

- **She Celebrates Herself:** She doesn't wait for someone else to acknowledge her wins. Whether it's a promotion, a great hair day, or just getting through a tough week, she cheers herself on.

- **She Takes Risks:** Confidence isn't based on always knowing the outcome—it's the trust that no matter what comes, you'll handle it with grace and strength. She says yes to the job she's scared of, the solo trip she's dreamed of, or the person who challenges her in the best way.

The Anthem: You Are The IT Girl

So here's what I need you to remember, my love: you are the IT Girl. You are the woman who rises from the ashes, who reclaims her light, who refuses to shrink for anyone. You are not the sum of your heartbreaks—you are the masterpiece created from them.

The IT Girl isn't just confident because of how she looks or what she has. She's confident because she knows who she is. She's the woman who can walk into any room and own it— not because she needs validation, but because she already validated herself.

I want to circle back on Confidence at a deeper level. Allow me to rampage a bit.

Confidence As A Way Of Life

Confidence is not synonymous with walking into a room and thinking you're better than everyone else—it's the quiet certainty that you belong there, without needing external validation. It's the quiet assurance that your value isn't up for negotiation. The IT Girl doesn't shrink herself to fit into someone else's story. She writes her own, in bold ink, and invites the right people to be a part of it.

Confidence isn't loud, but it is powerful. It's the subtle way you hold your head high, the way you choose your words carefully but never apologetically, and the way you're unafraid to take up space. Confidence whispers, "I know who I am, and I'm not here to convince you."

The Foundation: Self-Trust

Confidence starts with self-trust. It's not the kind of trust you place in others—the friend who always remembers your birthday or the partner who says the right things. This is deeper. It's the trust that you can rely on yourself—your instincts, your decisions, and your ability to recover when life throws a curveball that leaves you breathless. Self-trust is the quiet but resolute belief that, no matter what, you'll figure it out. Look in the mirror and see not just a reflection but the proof of resilience, courage, and the undeniable truth: you are enough.

Building that kind of unwavering belief isn't something you stumble into. It's cultivated, nurtured, and earned through action. Confidence isn't a gift some people are lucky to be born with—it's the result of showing up for yourself, day after day, even when it feels like the world is working against you.

The Power Of Keeping Promises To Yourself

Here's where the magic starts: promises. Not the grand, sweeping gestures we're so quick to make for others but the small, quiet commitments we make to ourselves. It's saying, "Tomorrow, I'll wake up early and go for that run," and actually doing it. It's vowing to prioritize your peace and following through by blocking that number you've been debating about for weeks. Every time you keep a promise to yourself, you're not just completing a task—you're casting a vote for the person you want to become.

Think of self-trust as a muscle. Every time you keep a promise, you're strengthening it, and every time you break one, you're weakening it. But here's the beautiful part: muscles can always be rebuilt. It doesn't matter how many times you've fallen short in the past. The moment you decide to honor even the smallest commitment to yourself, you're beginning the work of restoration.

Start Small, Think Big

The key to building self-trust is starting small. Forget the big, sweeping resolutions for a moment—those grand promises to transform overnight. Confidence is built in the micro-decisions, the ones that seem so insignificant they're easy to dismiss. It's choosing to take a five-minute walk when you promised yourself you'd move your body today. It's saying no to plans that drain your energy, even if the guilt of declining lingers in your chest for a moment. It's standing in the mirror each morning and whispering, "I am enough," even when it feels more like hope than belief.

These small actions might feel inconsequential at first, but over time, they compound. Each one sends a message to your subconscious: "I can count on myself." And that message is transformative. Because once you start believing in your own reliability, the world begins to feel less intimidating. Decisions become easier. Risks feel less risky. And the opinions of others start to matter a little less.

Reinforcing The Message: "I'm Worth It"

Thing about this: every time you honor a promise to yourself, it's like depositing a coin into the bank of self-trust. At first, the balance might be small, barely noticeable. But with each deposit—each boundary upheld, each goal met, each moment of self-care—the balance grows. And as it grows, so does your confidence. Not the flashy, performative kind that seeks validation from others, but the quiet, steady assurance that you are worthy of your own time, energy, and respect.

Think about the last time you broke a promise to yourself. Maybe it was skipping that workout you'd planned or ignoring the gut feeling that told you to walk away from a situation. How did it feel? Likely disappointing. Maybe even disempowering. That's the cost of self-betrayal—it erodes the foundation of trust you're trying to build. But the reverse is equally true. Each time you follow through, even in the smallest way, you're sending a powerful message: "I'm worth it. My goals, my peace, my happiness—they matter."

The Domino Effect Of Self-Trust

What's fascinating about self-trust is how contagious it is. The more you trust yourself, the more others will trust and respect you too. It's a ripple effect. When you walk into a room with the quiet confidence of someone who knows their worth, people notice. They may not be able to articulate it, but they'll feel it. Your energy will speak volumes before you say a single word.

This confidence doesn't just transform how others perceive you—it transforms how you perceive the world. Suddenly, opportunities you once felt unworthy of pursuing feel within reach. Conversations you avoided because of fear of rejection become less daunting. You stop waiting for permission to take up space because you've given it to yourself.

Practical Steps To Build Self-Trust

1. **Start With Micro-Promises**: Choose one small, manageable promise to keep each day. It might be drinking a glass of water in the morning or writing down one thing you're grateful for. Start small but stay consistent.

2. **Track Your Wins**: Keep a journal of the promises you've kept. Seeing your progress on paper reinforces your belief in your own reliability.

3. **Celebrate Yourself**: Acknowledge every step, no matter how small. Every promise kept is a reason to celebrate, so give yourself credit.

What Happens When You Trust Yourself

So, what's on the other side of self-trust? Freedom. Freedom from overthinking every decision because you believe in your ability to handle the outcome. Freedom from needing constant reassurance because you're your own greatest cheerleader. Freedom from the fear of failure because you know you'll pick yourself up and try again.

Self-trust also changes how you approach relationships. When you trust yourself, you stop relying on others to validate your worth. You enter partnerships from a place of strength, not neediness. You set boundaries without fear because you know you'll be okay, even if someone walks away. And you attract people who value you for who you are, not what you can do for them.

The Unshakable Belief

Here's the most beautiful part of self-trust: it's unshakable. Once you've built it, no one can take it away from you. Life will still throw its punches, and people may still disappoint you, but self-trust will be your anchor. It's the voice that says, "No matter what happens, I've got me." And that voice? It's the foundation of a life that feels as good as it looks.

So start small. Keep a promise to yourself today, no matter how tiny. Block that number. Go for that walk. Say no to the plan that doesn't light you up. And as you do, remember this: every act of self-trust is a declaration of your worth. Every small step is a giant leap toward the confident, radiant, unstoppable version of you that's waiting to emerge.

The Reminder You Need To Cultivate Your IT Girl Confidence

Confidence Isn't Reserved For The Boldest Or Loudest

True confidence doesn't mean being the loudest voice in the room or dominating every conversation. It's a quiet power, a steady flame that doesn't flicker even in a storm. The IT Girl knows this. She understands that confidence doesn't demand attention; it commands respect. It grows with intentionality, nurtured by choices that align with who you are and who you're becoming.

1. Redefine Your Narrative (Let's Talk About This Again). Stop telling yourself stories that shrink you. Replace "I'm not good enough" with "I'm learning and growing every day." Confidence starts in your mind, with the narratives you choose to believe. Rewrite the script. Make it one where you're the lead character, not a supporting role. Your story isn't one of survival; it's one of triumph.

The IT Girl knows that self-doubt isn't her truth; it's just a chapter. She doesn't ignore the doubts when they creep in—she faces them. She turns every "I can't" into "What if I can?" Every moment of uncertainty becomes an opportunity to rewrite her inner dialogue. And that's where confidence begins: not with being without flaws, but with persistence.

Exercise: Think of a narrative you've been repeating about yourself that holds you back. Write it down. Now, rewrite it in a way that empowers you. Turn "I always mess things up" into "I learn and grow from every experience." Watch how this simple shift changes your perspective.

Now it's time to speak to yourself nicely. Change some of those old repeating negative thoughts towards yourself to something positive even if you do not believe it right now.

_____

_____

_____

_____

_____

_____

_____

_____

_____

_____

_____

_____

_____

_____

_____

_____

_____

_____

_____

_____

_____

_____

_____

_____

2. Prioritize Self-Care

Confidence and self-care go hand in hand. When you treat yourself like someone who matters, you start to believe it. Self-care isn't just bubble baths and face masks; it's setting boundaries, eating nourishing foods, and getting enough rest. It's investing in your mental, physical, and emotional health. The IT Girl's self-care is not tied to indulgence—it's a practice of intention and self-respect.

She understands that prioritizing herself is not selfish—it's necessary. When you pour into yourself, you're better equipped to pour into others. Confidence grows when you know you're taking care of the vessel that carries you through life.

Action Step: Take an inventory of your current self-care practices. Are they intentional, or are they reactive? Schedule one hour this week to do something purely for you—whether it's taking a long walk, or cooking your favorite meal. Use this time to recharge and reconnect with yourself.

3. Dress The Part

Let's not underestimate the power of dressing for the life you want. The IT Girl doesn't wear clothes; she wears confidence. Whether it's a power blazer, a well-fitting pair of jeans, or a dress that makes you feel unstoppable, your wardrobe should be an extension of your self-assurance. Clothing is her armor, not her identity. She wears pieces that reflect her values— strong, unapologetic, and uniquely her.

Dressing the part has nothing to do with labels or trends—it's a reflection of intention and self-expression. The IT Girl curates her wardrobe to align with her aspirations. She knows that how she presents herself to the world is a reflection of how she feels about herself.

Try This: The next time you're feeling low on confidence, put on your favorite outfit—the one that makes you walk a little taller. Notice how this small change impacts your mood and mindset.

4. Speak With Intention

Your words are your power. Speak clearly, confidently, and without apology. Confidence is not based on dominating a conversation—it's the ability to contribute with intention and impact. The IT Girl chooses her words carefully, knowing they carry weight. Words are not filler; they're a declaration. When the IT Girl speaks, she's not afraid of silence—she uses it to amplify her presence.

Speaking with intention means being mindful of what you say and how you say it. It's pausing before responding, ensuring your words align with your values. Confidence grows when you use your voice to reflect your truth.

Practice This: The next time you're in a conversation, focus on listening fully before you speak. When you respond, do so with clarity and purpose. Notice how this changes the dynamic of the interaction.

5. Celebrate Your Wins

Big or small, celebrate your achievements. Did you finally make it to the gym after weeks of putting it off? Celebrate. Did you nail that presentation at work? Celebrate. Confidence grows when you acknowledge your progress, no matter how minor it may seem.

The IT Girl treats every milestone as a step in the right direction. Progress is her anthem, and celebration is her chorus. She knows that recognizing her achievements has nothing to do with seeking external validation—it's a reflection of her own growth and self-affirmation.

Create A Ritual: At the end of each day, write down one thing you accomplished. It could be as simple as getting eight hours of sleep or as big as completing a project. Over time, this practice will train your mind to focus on your wins rather than your shortcomings.

Overcoming Confidence Killers

Even the most self-assured woman faces moments of doubt. Confidence isn't a permanent state; it's a skill, one that's constantly honed by recognizing and addressing the factors that undermine it. The IT Girl doesn't pretend she's immune to insecurity—she acknowledges it, confronts it, and rises above it. Here's how she tackles the most common confidence killers and why mastering them is a lifelong commitment:

1. Comparison

Comparison is the thief of joy, and it's a trap that's easier to fall into than ever before. Social media scrolls can make it seem like everyone else is living a flawless, effortless life while you're stuck in the grind. But the IT Girl knows this: someone else's glow doesn't dim your shine.

She refuses to measure her success against someone else's highlight reel. Instead, she focuses on her own journey, her own wins, and her own growth. Her mantra? "Her success is not my failure." Every time she feels the pull of comparison, she grounds herself by asking, "What am I proud of today?"

Comparison is sneaky because it often masquerades as motivation. It's easy to think, "If she can do it, why can't I?" But this mindset can quickly spiral into self-doubt. The IT Girl flips the script by using others' achievements as inspiration rather than a benchmark for her worth.

Reframe Your Thinking: When you catch yourself comparing, shift the focus inward. Instead of thinking, "Why don't I have that?" ask, "What's something I've accomplished that makes me proud?" This small mental pivot can help you appreciate your unique path.

Practical Tip: Unfollow accounts that make you feel inadequate and curate a digital space filled with positivity and empowerment. Surround yourself with content that uplifts and motivates rather than triggers comparison.

2. Fear Of Failure

Failure is often painted as the enemy of success, but the IT Girl sees it differently. For her, failure isn't the opposite of success—it's part of the process. Each misstep is a lesson, a stepping stone toward greater confidence and growth. She doesn't view failure as a personal flaw but as evidence that she's trying, learning, and evolving.

Her perspective? **"If I'm not failing, I'm not trying hard enough."** Every stumble is a badge of courage, proof that she had the bravery to step outside her comfort zone. And she knows that the true failure lies not in falling but in refusing to rise again.

Failure can feel like a full stop, but the IT Girl treats it as a comma—a pause, not an end. She views every setback as an opportunity to reassess, recalibrate, and try again with newfound wisdom.

Actionable Insight: Reframe failure as feedback. When something doesn't go as planned, ask yourself, "What can I learn from this? How will this make me stronger next time?" Celebrate the effort, not just the outcome.

Practical Tip: Create a "failure journal." Document your missteps and, next to each one, write what you learned. Over time, you'll see that failure isn't something to fear but a stepping stone to success.

3. Negative Self-Talk

The way you speak to yourself matters more than you think. The IT Girl is keenly aware that her internal dialogue shapes her reality. When she catches herself spiraling into self-criticism, she pauses and asks, "Would I say this to my best friend?" If the answer is no, she rewrites the script.

Her inner voice isn't a critic; it's a coach. She replaces harsh judgments with words of encouragement. Instead of saying, "I'll never get this right," she says, "I'm figuring it out, and that's enough." This shift transforms her inner dialogue into her greatest ally.

Negative self-talk can often feel like second nature, but the IT Girl knows that changing the narrative is essential for growth.

She's intentional about nurturing a kind and supportive inner voice.

Practice This: The next time you're tempted to criticize yourself, pause and reframe. Turn "I'm so bad at this" into "I'm still learning, and that's okay." Watch how this simple change impacts your confidence.

Practical Tip: Keep a "self-talk tracker." Each time you catch a negative thought, write it down and rewrite it in a positive light. Over time, this practice will retrain your brain to default to self-compassion.

Overcoming confidence killers is not really about eliminating doubt altogether—it's the mastery of navigating it with grace and resilience. The IT Girl knows that confidence isn't static; it's dynamic, evolving with every choice, every challenge, and every victory.

Confidence Rituals

Confidence isn't built overnight, but daily rituals can help you strengthen it. The IT Girl incorporates simple yet transformative practices into her routine to reinforce her self-belief. These rituals act as touchstones, reminding her of her worth and her ability to handle whatever comes her way.

Morning Affirmations

Start your day with affirmations that remind you of your worth. Words have power, and speaking positivity into existence sets the tone for your day. The IT Girl begins her mornings with declarations like:

- "I am capable, resilient, and worthy of success."
- "I trust myself to make the best decisions for my life."
- "I am enough, exactly as I am."

She looks herself in the mirror as she speaks these affirmations, allowing the words to sink in and take root. Over time, what might feel forced becomes second nature.

Try This: Choose one affirmation that resonates with you and repeat it daily for a week. Notice how it shifts your mindset and energy.

Journaling

Confidence grows in the quiet moments of reflection. The IT Girl uses journaling as a tool to deepen her self-awareness and track her progress. By putting pen to paper, she creates space to celebrate her wins, process her doubts, and set her intentions. Feel free to use the crowned journal I created (hint hint) on Opals & Carats.com.

Prompts To Explore:

- "What's one thing I'm proud of today?"
- "What fear can I let go of?"
- "How did I show up for myself this week?"

Journaling isn't just a practice of reflection—it's an act of recognition. It's a way to honor your growth and reaffirm your inherent worth.

Power Poses

It may sound silly, but your posture affects your mindset. The IT Girl knows the science behind power poses—simple physical stances that can boost confidence and reduce stress.

Before a big meeting, a challenging conversation, or any moment that requires courage, she takes a few minutes to stand tall, shoulders back, and head high. This small act shifts her energy, making her feel strong and capable.

Try This: Stand in a power pose for two minutes before your next big moment. Feel the shift in your energy and notice how it impacts your confidence.

What's extraordinary about confidence is its contagious nature. When the IT Girl radiates self-assurance, she inspires those around her to do the same. Her energy creates a ripple effect, encouraging others to step into their power.

This is not tied to perfection; it's about authenticity. The IT Girl's confidence comes not from being flawless but from owning her flaws. She embraces her humanity, and in doing so, she gives others permission to do the same.

Remember This: Confidence isn't about never experiencing doubt—it's the power to move forward despite it. It's the courage to show up, even when you're scared, and the trust that you'll figure it out along the way.

What Confidence In Action Looks Like

Confidence isn't a feeling; it's a practice. Here's how the IT Girl puts her confidence into action:

Say No Without Guilt

The IT Girl doesn't overcommit or people-please. She says no to what doesn't serve her, knowing that every "no" makes space for a better "yes."

Her boundaries are her sanctuary. Saying no isn't rejection; it's self-preservation.

Take Risks

Confidence thrives outside your comfort zone. Whether it's speaking up in a meeting, trying a new hobby, or asking for what you deserve, the IT Girl knows that growth requires risk.

Her motto: "Comfort never creates greatness."

Surround Yourself With Support

Your circle matters. Confidence flourishes in an environment of encouragement. The IT Girl surrounds herself with people who inspire her, challenge her, and celebrate her.

She curates her circle with care, knowing that energy is contagious.

The Confidence Mindset

The IT Girl understands that confidence doesn't mean never experiencing doubt—it means pushing forward despite it. Confidence is a mindset that says, "I'm allowed to take up space. I'm allowed to be imperfect. I'm allowed to learn as I go."

This mindset is built on the foundation of self-love. The IT Girl doesn't wait for external validation to feel good about herself. She validates her own worth every single day.

Her confidence is an act of rebellion against a world that profits from insecurity.

The IT Girl knows that confidence isn't defined by being without flaws—it's rooted in presence. It's the power of owning who you are, flaws and all, and showing up anyway.

And confidence isn't just how she moves; it's how she lives. And it's available to you, too.

The Role Of Self-Love

Self-love isn't just an indulgence; it's the compass that guides your entire life. Without it, even the most dazzling achievements feel hollow, the most loving gestures fall flat, and the boundaries you need remain invisible to those who should honor them. It's not something you stumble upon on a good day or pull out in moments of crisis. Self-love is a practice—a non-negotiable commitment to yourself that permeates every decision, interaction, and relationship.

When self-love takes root, it reshapes everything. You stop chasing relationships to validate your existence. You stop apologizing for the space you take up. You stop staying in places—physical, emotional, or relational—that make you feel small because self-love demands that you stand tall. Even when no one else sees it, self-love is there, holding you up.

Let's get one thing straight: self-love isn't the polished self-care Instagram aesthetic of facemasks and candlelit baths. Those are nice, but they're not the foundation. Real self-love is messy. It's how you treat yourself when no one's watching, the quiet decisions you make to protect your energy, honor your boundaries, and meet your needs. It's choosing yourself over and over again—especially when it's hard.

Self-love isn't one of those self-help platitudes you scribble down and forget about. It's the oxygen mask in the crash landing of life, the anchor when the tides of love and chaos try to carry you away. It's what your grandmother would have whispered in your ear after a heartbreak: *"You're already enough, my darling, so stop waiting for someone else to realize it."* But somehow, that wisdom gets buried under the noise of life—until one day, it isn't just advice; it's a lifeline.

And here's the secret no one tells you: self-love is the antidote to everything that's gone wrong in the love department. It's the quiet realization that nothing you've lost would have ever stayed if it truly belonged to you. It's looking at the wreckage of failed relationships and thinking, *Was I really supposed to shrink myself for that?* Self-love isn't loud or flashy; it's deliberate, like slipping into silk pajamas after a day that's asked too much of you. It's saying, *I choose me,* not out of arrogance, but because no one else can do it better.

The Lie That Love Requires Sacrifice

Here's the lie women have been fed for centuries: that love requires sacrifice. Sacrifice your dreams, your comfort, your boundaries—*and if you're not willing to do it, is it even real love?* It's the kind of myth that's embedded in every story ever told, from fairy tales to tragic romances, where the heroine gives up everything to be chosen by the hero. And for what? A castle she has to clean and a prince she has to teach how to respect her?

But love isn't supposed to feel like martyrdom. Love isn't an altar you kneel at while someone else stands tall. If someone's love feels like it's asking you to diminish yourself, that's not love—it's a trap wrapped in the language of affection. Self-love is the ability to stand in front of that altar and walk away, even if the world whispers that you're selfish for doing so.

The Mirror Test

There's a mirror test no one talks about, but it's the simplest way to measure the state of your self-love. Stand in front of a mirror, look yourself in the eyes, and ask: *Am I living for me or for them?* The answer will always reveal itself in the quiet discomfort that follows. If you hesitate, if the answer is muddled with excuses or justifications, then the truth is there, staring back at you.

Self-love is what turns that hesitation into certainty. It's what helps you look at that reflection and think, *I don't need to explain my worth to anyone—not even myself.* It's the kind of realization that feels like a weight lifting, not because the world gets easier, but because you've stopped carrying the unnecessary burden of proving your value.

The Truth About Walking Away

Every woman has had that moment. The one where she knows, deep in her gut, that she's staying somewhere she doesn't belong. Maybe it's a job, a relationship, or a version of herself that no longer fits. And yet, she stays because the fear of leaving feels greater than the pain of staying. But self-love whispers the hard truths we try to ignore: *You are allowed to leave the table when love is no longer being served.*

Walking away is the ultimate act of self-respect, and yet it's the one that feels most impossible. Why? Because leaving requires confronting the one thing we avoid at all costs: ourselves. When you strip away the noise, the excuses, and the distractions, you're left with the raw truth. Walking away has nothing to do with them; it's about you. It's about trusting that you deserve more than what you've been given and that there's something better waiting—if you're brave enough to reach for it.

The Power Of Saying No

There's a kind of magic in the word *no*. It's sharp, definitive, and freeing. But women are taught that *no* is a weapon to be wielded sparingly, as if using it too often will make us unlovable. Self-love turns that narrative on its head. *No* becomes a boundary, not a barrier. It's the quiet defiance of choosing yourself over the fear of disappointing someone else.

When you say *no* to what doesn't serve you, you're saying *yes* to what does. You're creating space for the things that align with your worth. And the best part? *No* doesn't require an explanation. It doesn't need to be softened or justified. Sometimes, the best answer is simply, *Because I said so.*

What Self-Love Feels Like

Self-love feels like coming home to yourself. It's the quiet peace of knowing that you don't need anyone else to validate your existence. It's the confidence to walk into a room without shrinking, to love without losing, and to leave without regret. It's not without its challenges, and it's not always easy. There will be days when the world feels too heavy and the mirror feels unkind. But even on those days, self-love is the whisper that says, *You're worth it.*

It feels like a soft bed after a hard day, like the freedom of a laugh that comes from your belly. It's choosing rest over overextension, boundaries over people-pleasing, and authenticity over approval. Self-love feels like a warm cup of tea on a cold day—or in the case of those who hate tea, like the satisfaction of something indulgent and entirely yours.

Why This Matters

Self-love is not the heart of building a fortress around your heart; it's about building a foundation under your feet. It's what allows you to navigate the chaos of life without losing yourself. It's the strength to stand tall in the face of rejection, the grace to forgive your past, and the courage to create a future that feels like your own.

Every time you choose yourself, you're rewriting the narrative that says your worth is tied to someone else's opinion. You're reclaiming the story that has always been yours to tell. And when you do that? That's when the real magic begins. Because self-love isn't just a destination—it's the journey that transforms everything along the way.

Recognizing When Self-Love is Missing

Sometimes, the absence of self-love isn't obvious. It doesn't always announce itself with bold declarations or glaring signs. Often, it's subtle—a slow erosion hidden under layers of people-pleasing, fear, and unresolved pain. Recognizing the void is the first step to filling it.

Here's how a lack of self-love can show up:

- You stay in situations that hurt you because leaving feels scarier than staying.

- You tolerate behavior that makes you feel unseen, unheard, or unworthy.

- You overextend yourself, hoping to earn love, approval, or validation.

- You put everyone else's needs ahead of your own until there's nothing left for you.

If any of this feels familiar, don't despair. Self-love is resilient. It's always within reach. The beauty of self-love is that it's not something you have to find; it's something you can choose— again and again.

How Self-Love Redefines Standards

When self-love becomes your foundation, your standards transform. You no longer settle for mediocrity in relationships, work, or life. You stop justifying red flags or compromising on your needs. Instead, you raise the bar—not out of arrogance but out of an unshakable understanding of your worth.

Self-love whispers, *You deserve effort. You deserve care. You deserve to feel chosen.* And if someone can't meet you at that level? Self-love gives you the strength to walk away, knowing that their inability to rise isn't a reflection of your worth but of their readiness.

Self-Love Is A Habit, Not A Destination

Contrary to what self-help books and Instagram captions might suggest, self-love isn't a finish line. It's not something you achieve once and keep forever. Self-love is a habit—a daily practice of showing up for yourself, even when it's hard.

Some days, self-love looks like saying no to plans that feel like obligations. Other days, it's walking away from a relationship that no longer serves you. It's in the small, unglamorous moments—choosing rest over hustle, speaking up when it's easier to stay silent, or forgiving yourself when you fall short. Building self-love is like building a muscle. It takes time, consistency, and a willingness to embrace discomfort. But the payoff? It's life-changing.

How Self-Love Transforms Relationships

Self-love is not merely a foundation; it's the very essence of how you move through life—the compass that keeps you grounded, even when everything else feels chaotic. It's the unapologetic embrace of who you are, standing fully in your power without shrinking or seeking permission for the space you take up. But let's be real: the concept of self-love can feel daunting, especially when relationships seem to demand so much of us. How do you love yourself in a world that often encourages self-sacrifice for the sake of others? How do you make self-love not just an idea, but a practice that transforms your relationships and, ultimately, your life?

Loving Without Losing Yourself

How many times have you felt like you were bending over backward to make a relationship work? Maybe you find yourself asking questions like:

- *"Am I being too demanding?"*

- *"If I just compromise a little more, maybe he'll finally get it."*

- *"Why does it feel like I'm carrying the emotional weight of this relationship?"*

These aren't fleeting thoughts; they're signs that your boundaries are blurred, and your sense of self is taking a backseat. It's easy to fall into the trap of over-giving in relationships, especially when society glorifies the idea of selflessness as the ultimate expression of love. But the truth is: love that requires you to abandon yourself isn't love—it's compromise masquerading as connection.

True love doesn't demand that you pour from an empty cup. It's a partnership where both people's needs, desires, and boundaries are honored. If you're constantly giving from a place of depletion, you'll find yourself exhausted and resentful, no matter how much you care about the other person.

The Mirror Effect: What Your Relationship Reflects About You

It's a hard pill to swallow, but your relationships often reflect how you feel about yourself. If your inner dialogue is filled with doubt, self-criticism, or insecurity, those feelings will manifest in your interactions. You'll find yourself tolerating behaviors that mirror your internal struggles—whether it's a partner's dismissiveness, lack of consistency, or emotional unavailability.

Let's look at a scenario. You're dating someone who constantly cancels plans, rarely texts first, and makes you feel like an afterthought. Instead of addressing it, you tell yourself things like, "He's just busy," or "I'm probably being too sensitive." But ask yourself this: would you encourage your best friend to stay in a relationship like this? If the answer is no, why are you accepting it for yourself?

Solution: Define what respect, attention, and care look like for you. Be as specific as possible. Maybe respect means they follow through on their commitments. Maybe care means they're engaged in your passions and show genuine curiosity about your life. Write these standards down. Next, take an honest look at your relationship and ask, "Am I getting what I need?" If the answer is no, it's time to have a conversation. Frame it around your values: "This is what's important to me. How do you feel about aligning on this?" If they're unwilling or dismissive, it's a sign that they may not be able to meet you at the level you deserve.

Breaking The Cycle Of Seeking Validation

Many of us are taught, directly or indirectly, that love is something you earn. If you're accommodating enough, attractive enough, or agreeable enough, you'll be worthy of love. This belief sets the stage for a dangerous pattern of seeking validation from others instead of cultivating it within yourself.

Think about how exhausting it is to look for approval in every interaction. You overanalyze texts, replay arguments in your head, and hinge your happiness on how your partner treats you on any given day. This cycle doesn't just drain you; it reinforces the idea that your worth is conditional.

Solution: The antidote to external validation is building an internal reservoir of self-worth. Start each morning with affirmations that ground you in your value. Write down three things you love about yourself and three qualities you're proud of. These could be as simple as "I'm thoughtful" or "I handled a stressful situation well yesterday." At the end of each day, reflect on small wins or moments you showed up for yourself. Over time, this practice retrains your brain to seek fulfillment from within rather than from others.

Let's start this now (or tomorrow morning come back to this page and start)....

_____

_____

_____

_____

_____

_____

_____

_____

_____

_____

_____

_____

_____

_____

_____

_____

_____

_____

_____

_____

_____

_____

_____

_____

When you catch yourself seeking approval, pause and ask, "What am I hoping to feel? How can I provide that feeling for myself instead?" For example, if you're fishing for compliments because you want to feel beautiful, take time to dress up for yourself or engage in activities that make you feel radiant. The more you meet your own needs, the less you'll depend on others to validate your existence.

Choosing Love, Not Chasing It

When you choose love rather than chase it, your entire perspective shifts. Chasing love often looks like bending over backward to prove your worth or trying to mold yourself into someone else's ideal. Choosing love, on the other hand, is rooted in intention. It's the clarity of knowing what you want, standing firm in your values, and having the courage to walk away from anything that doesn't align.

Solution: Reflect on the dynamics of your current or past relationships. Ask yourself: "Was I chasing their approval, or was I building something mutual?" If you notice patterns of overcompensating, take a step back. Start setting boundaries that reflect your needs. For instance, if you were always the one initiating plans in any relationship, pull back and observe how the other person responds. Healthy relationships should feel balanced, not like a one-sided effort.

Letting Go To Make Room For More

Letting go of relationships that no longer serve you is one of the most courageous acts of self-love. It's not just the act of walking away—it's the liberation of the hope, time, and emotional energy you once invested. It's painful, yes, but staying in a relationship that stunts your growth is far more damaging. This I want to remind you again of.

Building A Relationship That Reflects Your Worth

When you anchor yourself in self-love, your relationships transform. You're no longer afraid to voice your needs, set boundaries, or walk away from dynamics that don't honor you. Instead of seeking someone to complete you, you approach relationships as a whole person, ready to build a connection based on mutual respect and growth.

Self-Love As Liberation

Here's the magic of self-love: it frees you. It liberates you from the endless cycle of people-pleasing, the crushing weight of unspoken expectations, and the paralyzing fear of being alone. Self-love reminds you that your worth isn't negotiable. It's not up for debate, and anyone who doesn't see it? They're not your person.

Self-love gives you the courage to walk into any room with your head held high. It allows you to ask for what you need, say no to what doesn't serve you, and walk away from what hurts you. It's not arrogance; it's alignment—with your values, your goals, and your worth.

What Self-Love Asks Of You: The Unapologetic Truth

Self-love isn't the quiet type. It doesn't sit politely in the background, waiting for you to notice. It strides in confidently, unapologetically, commanding attention. Self-love declares: *You are enough*. Not when you lose weight, land a promotion, or find a partner. Right now. As you are. But here's the truth: arriving at self-love isn't effortless. It's messy. It's layered. And it requires work—the kind only you can do.

Self-love isn't about waiting for the right moment or seeking validation from someone else. It's the commitment to showing up for yourself, especially on the days when it feels impossible. It's the relentless act of choosing yourself, time and time again—because the alternative is losing yourself. And losing yourself? That's not an option.

The Hard Conversations

Why are you staying where you're not valued? Why are you chasing someone who won't stop running? Why are you dimming your light to make someone else more comfortable? These are the hard questions self-love demands you ask. And the answers? They're not easy. They force you to confront truths you've been avoiding.

Fear often whispers the excuses. Fear of being alone. Fear of regret. Fear of admitting you invested time and energy in something that isn't working. But if we're being honest: fear isn't a good enough reason to stay stuck. Self-love doesn't ask these questions to hurt you. It asks them to wake you up.

Here's the truth no one likes to hear: the right person—the right friends, the right relationships, the right career—will never make you feel like you have to fight for their respect or their time. If someone consistently makes you question your value, stop justifying their behavior. Stop trying to fix them. People show you who they are; your job is to believe them.

Highlight This: If you find yourself explaining why you deserve basic decency, they're not listening. And you shouldn't have to keep shouting.

The Courage To Let Go

Let's not sugarcoat this: letting go is brutal. It's walking away from the vision of what could have been, from the hope that things will change, and from the familiarity of what you know—even if what you know is draining you. The fear of letting go is rooted in questions like: *What if I never find better? What if I've made a mistake? What if this is as good as it gets?*

But holding on to something that depletes you? That's worse. Walking away isn't giving up. It's refusing to accept less than you deserve. It's reclaiming your energy, your peace, your life. It's saying, "This no longer aligns with who I am becoming, and I choose me."

Here's another truth: the people and opportunities meant for you will never require you to break yourself to keep them. If you're constantly bending, twisting, and shrinking to fit into someone else's world, what are you losing in the process?

Highlight This: Letting go doesn't mean giving up—it's the intentional act of making space for what truly aligns, for what's better.

Takie Up Space

Let's talk about the lifelong conditioning that tells women to apologize for existing. Apologize for speaking too much, for being too ambitious, for taking up room—literally and metaphorically. Self-love doesn't just suggest you stop apologizing—it insists on it. It's not just about being seen; it's about claiming your space, your voice, and your power unapologetically.

Taking up space means setting the standard for how others treat you. It's standing tall and saying, "I belong here," without waiting for someone else to agree. And here's the reality: there will always be people who think you're too much. Too opinionated, too bold, too confident. Let them. That's their discomfort to deal with, not yours.

Highlight This: You don't have to apologize for being everything someone else can't handle.

The Power Of Enough

Society thrives on telling you that you're not enough. It markets products, programs, and promises all designed to make you feel like you're one step away from worthiness. Lose ten pounds, buy this cream, land this job, get this partner—then you'll finally be enough. But here's the untold truth: you don't have to earn your worth. You were born with it.

Enough doesn't mean settling. It doesn't mean staying stagnant. Enough means recognizing that you are valuable right now, in this moment. It means growing because you want to, not because you feel like you have to. And anyone who makes you feel like you're not enough? They don't belong in your life.

Highlight This: Enough isn't something you achieve; it's something you realize.

Owning Your Worth

Owning your worth is an act of rebellion in a world that profits from your insecurities. It's not about striving for perfection—it's about embracing authenticity. It's the power of standing in your truth and declaring, "This is who I am. Take it or leave it." And the right people? They'll always take it.

The world will test you. It will throw people and situations your way that make you question everything. Self-love is what anchors you. It's what allows you to walk away from what doesn't serve you and walk toward what does. It's what reminds you, again and again, that your worth isn't up for debate.

Owning your worth means you stop chasing. You stop convincing. You stop bending yourself into a version of someone you think others will accept. You start attracting people and opportunities that align with the truth of who you are.

Highlight This: Self-love isn't a luxury; it's a necessity. Protect it fiercely.

When Self-Love Becomes Second Nature

Here's the magic of self-love: once it takes root, it doesn't just transform how you see yourself—it transforms everything. It changes how you move through the world. You stop second-guessing your decisions. You stop worrying about who likes you or who doesn't because you genuinely like yourself. And that? That's the foundation of everything.

You begin to choose differently. You say no without guilt. You say yes without hesitation. You align yourself with people who uplift you, not because they validate you, but because they respect you. And in those moments, you realize something extraordinary: the love you were looking for was never outside of you. It was always within.

Highlight This: The greatest love story you'll ever write is the one you have with yourself. Make it epic.

So take up space. Let go of what's holding you back. Own your worth. Not because anyone else says you should, but because you deserve to. And when the world tries to tell you otherwise, roar loud enough to remind it who you are.

The Role of Self-Love In Your Future

If there's one thing to take away, let it be this: self-love isn't optional. It's the foundation for everything you want to build—whether it's a thriving career, a fulfilling relationship, or a peaceful life. Without it, even the most beautiful dreams crumble.

So, let today be the day you choose yourself. Not halfway. Not conditionally. Fully. Let it be the day you stop waiting for permission to prioritize your happiness. Let it be the day you look in the mirror and say, "I am enough," and truly believe it. Because you are. And when you fully embrace that truth, the world will have no choice but to reflect it back to you.

Valuing Your Standards: The Unapologetic Art Of Not Settling

Standards aren't just preferences—they're the blueprint for your life. They're not whimsical or negotiable; they're the rules you've written for how you deserve to be treated and what you'll allow in your orbit. Your standards are a bold declaration of self-respect, even when the world calls you "too picky" or "difficult." But here's the off-record secret: standards aren't the problem. Accepting less than them is.

Too many women are taught to fear their standards. The whispers of *What if no one measures up?* and *Maybe I'm asking for too much* echo in their minds until they shrink, settle, and lower the bar so low that anyone can crawl over it. But the truth: your standards are not the issue. Your fear of enforcing them is.

The Fear Of Standards

Let's address the elephant in the room. There's this pervasive fear that having standards means you'll end up alone. But think about this: would you rather be alone, standing tall in your power, or surrounded by people who chip away at your self-worth? Standards aren't walls; they're doors. They filter out the unworthy and let the right people in.

The idea that high standards equate to loneliness is one of the greatest lies ever told. The reality? Lowering your standards doesn't guarantee connection—it guarantees dissatisfaction. Every time you accept less than what you deserve, you send a message to yourself: *My needs aren't important.* And that's a dangerous narrative to live by.

Secret To Remember: Your standards aren't a prison; they're a palace. Only those who can appreciate their value should be allowed entry.

Standards Are Not Negotiable

Here's the thing about standards: they're not suggestions or recommendations. They're boundaries wrapped in self-respect. They're not there to please others or make you likable. They're there to protect you, to ensure that you're living a life aligned with your values and worth.

Think about this: would you negotiate the quality of your friendships? Would you compromise on the respect you receive in a relationship? Of course not. So why treat your standards as if they're optional?

When someone asks you to lower your standards, what they're really saying is, "Can you make it easier for me to give you less?" And the answer to that is simple: no. The right people won't ask you to shrink yourself to accommodate their comfort.

Secret To Remember: Anyone who asks you to lower your standards is showing you they're not ready to rise to meet them.

The Courage To Walk Away

Having standards means you'll have to walk away sometimes. And between me and you: walking away is hard. It's painful to leave behind something or someone you've invested in. But settling? That's even harder. When you stay in situations that don't meet your standards, you're not saving yourself from heartbreak. You're prolonging it.

Walking away shouldn't be tied to arrogance or playing hard to get—it's an act of self-preservation. It's the realization that you deserve more and the refusal to compromise your peace temporary convenience. And while the world might label you "too much," let them. Better to be "too much" than to accept too little.

Secret To Remember: Walking away doesn't mean you're giving up. It means you're clearing the way for what's right.

Standards Are A Reflection Of Self-Love

Your standards are a mirror of how you see yourself. When you have high standards, you're telling the world, "I value myself enough to expect the best." When you lower them, you're sending the opposite message: "I'll settle for less because I don't believe I deserve more."

Think about the areas where your standards are slipping. Is it in relationships? Work? Friendships? The pattern reveals how you're valuing yourself. If you're making excuses for bad behavior, tolerating disrespect, or staying silent when you should speak up, it's time to reevaluate. Your standards aren't just about what you accept from others; they're about how you treat yourself.

Secret To Remember: The way you enforce your standards is a direct reflection of how much you love yourself.

Standards Are Freedom, Not Restriction

There's a misconception that having high standards makes life harder, but the truth is, standards simplify everything. They weed out the wrong people and opportunities before you waste your time. They save you from heartbreak, regret, and resentment. They ensure that what you allow into your life aligns with what you truly want.

Standards give you freedom. Freedom from settling, from second-guessing, from wondering if you're asking for too much. Because when you're clear about what you deserve, you're not afraid to say no to anything that doesn't measure up.

Secret To Remember: Standards don't complicate your life; they streamline it.

When Standards Become Second Nature

The beauty of valuing your standards is that over time, they become second nature. You stop questioning if you're asking for too much. You stop explaining why your needs matter. You start living in alignment with your worth, and everything else falls into place.

You find yourself walking away from people who don't treat you well without hesitation. You say no to opportunities that don't align with your goals. You stop entertaining situations that don't meet your expectations because you know there's something better out there.

And the best part? You realize that your standards were never the problem. They were the solution all along.

Secret To Remember: The life you deserve starts with the standards you set. Protect them, honor them, and never apologize for them.

So, stop shrinking. Stop settling. Stop lowering the bar just to make others comfortable. Your standards aren't just a part of who you are—they're a testament to everything you believe you deserve. And you, my dear, deserve nothing less than extraordinary.

Value Your Standards

Standards aren't just preferences—they're the blueprint for your life. They're the unshakable framework that defines not just how you want to be treated, but how you're going to live. They're not the "maybe's" of your existence; they're the must-haves. They're your red velvet rope, the kind you see outside exclusive clubs—the line that separates those who are in from those who are out. And yes, they're unapologetic. Because why should you apologize for expecting the best for yourself?

The thing about standards is they're not there to make others comfortable. They're there to make sure you're not wasting your time. Yet, so many of us feel guilty for having them, like we're asking for too much just by having a baseline for respect, effort, and alignment. Let me tell you something that's rarely said aloud: standards aren't the problem. Settling is.

Somewhere along the way, we were taught to fear our standards. To see them as obstacles to happiness rather than the compass pointing us toward it. There's this nagging voice whispering, *What if no one measures up? What if you end up alone?* But let's unpack that, shall we? Would you rather be alone, living in your truth, or surrounded by people who drain you, diminish you, and don't deserve you?

Standards aren't walls to keep people out—they're doors that only open for the right ones. And if someone calls you "picky" or "difficult," it's probably because they don't want to rise to meet your level. Let them stay where they are. You're busy building a life that's worthy of you.

Take the friend who waited years for the kind of partner she knew she deserved. Let's call her Chloe. Chloe had heard it all: "You're too selective," "You're looking for perfection," "You'll end up alone if you keep this up." But Chloe wasn't moved. She'd been in relationships before where she'd compromised, where she'd accepted half-hearted effort, and she'd promised herself she'd never do it again. Chloe's standards weren't about finding someone who ticked every box on a superficial checklist; they were about alignment. She wanted a partner who showed up, who communicated, who made her feel safe without her having to fight for it.

For years, she'd attend weddings alone, fielding whispers from well-meaning relatives and friends. "Have you tried dating apps?" "What about giving that guy a chance? You're not getting any younger, you know." Still, Chloe waited. She'd rather spend another year single than another moment with someone who made her feel like she was asking for too much.

And then he arrived. Not as a grand spectacle or a whirlwind romance, but as a quiet, steady presence. He didn't flinch at her standards; he admired them. He showed up on time, listened when she spoke, and never made her question where she stood. Love with him wasn't about proving or persuading. It was about being. Now, Chloe is in a relationship where love doesn't feel like a negotiation—it feels like home.

Then there's the colleague, Ava, who turned down a job offer that most people would've jumped at. On paper, it seemed flawless—prestige, a six-figure salary, and a title that would make anyone's LinkedIn profile shine. But Ava saw the red flags. During the interview, her future boss made snide remarks about work-life balance, and she noticed how exhausted the team looked. Ava's gut told her this wasn't right, but she still wrestled with the decision. People told her she was crazy to walk away. "Do you know how many people would kill for this opportunity?" they said. But Ava knew herself. She knew that no paycheck could compensate for being miserable every day.

It wasn't easy. For months after declining the offer, Ava wondered if she'd made a mistake. But then, seemingly out of nowhere, another opportunity arose—a smaller company with a mission that aligned seamlessly with her values. The role allowed her creativity to shine, and her boss treated her like a partner rather than an employee. Ava's decision to say no to what looked good on paper led her to something that felt right in her soul. She didn't just find a job; she found fulfillment. High standards don't lead to loneliness—they lead to fulfillment.

But let's get real: holding those standards can feel lonely at times. You might find yourself staring at your phone, wondering why someone hasn't called back. You might feel the sting of walking into a party alone or answering the "Why are you still single?" questions at family dinners. Those moments? They're tests, not indictments. Tests of whether you're willing to hold out for what you know you deserve.

Standards aren't a "Choose Your Own Adventure" novel. They're the rules of engagement for your life. They're non-negotiable because they're rooted in your self-worth. And here's the truth: people who care about you will never ask you to compromise them. If someone's asking you to lower the bar, what they're really saying is, "Can you make it easier for me to give you less?" The answer? No. Absolutely not.

Would you negotiate respect in a relationship? Or the integrity of a friendship? Of course not. Your standards aren't there to be bent or broken—they're there to ensure that your life is built on a foundation of mutual respect, alignment, and authenticity. And anyone who sees them as "optional" is telling you loud and clear that they're not ready to meet you where you are.

Let's put it this way about walking away: it's both the hardest and most powerful thing you'll ever do. You've invested time, energy, maybe even love into something—or someone—that just doesn't fit anymore. And quite frankly: walking away doesn't come without second-guessing. You'll replay the good moments on a loop and question if you're being unreasonable. But staying in something that drains you? That's the real heartbreak.

Let's say you're dating someone who's nice—nice enough. They're polite, they show up, but they're just... there. You know deep down that this isn't it, but you stay because they're nice. Here's the truth: nice isn't enough. Respect, effort, and emotional availability are. Staying with someone who's "nice enough" isn't a compromise—it's settling. And settling is the slow erosion of your self-respect.

Your standards are a mirror, reflecting how much you value yourself. When you have high standards, you're saying to the world, "I know my worth." Lower them, and you're sending the opposite message: "I'll settle because I don't believe I deserve more." Think about the areas where your standards might be slipping. Is it in your relationships? Your career? Your friendships? The patterns speak volumes about how you're treating yourself. If you're constantly making excuses for others, tolerating disrespect, or staying silent when you should speak up, it's time to take a step back.

Having standards doesn't complicate life; it simplifies it. They're not restrictions; they're a roadmap. They save you from wasting time on the wrong people, the wrong jobs, the wrong opportunities. They make decisions clearer, quicker, and infinitely more aligned with who you are.

Think about the decisions you've made that brought peace into your life. Maybe it was declining an invitation to an event that felt more like an obligation than a joy. Maybe it was leaving a job where your contributions went unnoticed. Or maybe it was ending a relationship that left you feeling more alone than when you were actually by yourself. Each of those decisions was powered by your standards, even if you didn't realize it at the time. They weren't about being difficult or demanding; they were about staying true to yourself.

When you live by your standards, something magical happens: life gets simpler. You stop wasting time on people who don't align with your values. You stop overthinking every text, every gesture, every relationship. You walk into rooms with your head high, knowing that the right people will gravitate toward you—not because you begged for their attention, but because they recognize your worth.

Your standards aren't just a part of who you are—they're your crown. They're the invisible line you draw to protect your energy, your peace, and your heart. And when you honor them, the world adjusts. You stop chasing people who don't prioritize you. You stop justifying your needs to those who don't care to understand them. Instead, you create space for the things and people that truly belong in your life.

The truth is, high standards don't push people away; they attract the right ones. The ones who see your worth without you needing to explain it. The ones who don't flinch at your expectations because they're already striving to meet them. And isn't that what you deserve? Not someone who tolerates you, but someone who celebrates you. Someone who doesn't just meet your standards but exceeds them.

The life you deserve starts with the standards you set. So wear your crown proudly. Stand firm in what you know you deserve. And remember, you're not asking for too much. You're just asking the wrong people.

The Work: What To Do Next

1. **Define Your Standards**

    Write them down. Be specific. "I want someone who respects my time" isn't enough. What does respect look like to you? Is it showing up on time? Following through on promises? Putting in effort without being asked? Get clear on what you need, and don't apologize for it.

2. **Communicate Your Standards**

   People can't meet your expectations if they don't know what they are. Be upfront about what you need and why it matters. And if someone reacts poorly to your boundaries? That's not a reflection of your standards—it's a reflection of their inability to meet them.

3. **Hold Yourself Accountable**

   Standards mean nothing if you don't enforce them. It's not enough to say, "I won't tolerate disrespect." You have to act on it. When someone crosses a line, address it. If they keep crossing it, walk away.

4. **Surround Yourself With High-Standard People**

   The people in your life set the tone for what you accept. Surround yourself with friends who uplift you, partners who respect you, and mentors who inspire you. Their energy will reinforce your own.

5. **Practice Self-Compassion**

   This journey won't be without its challenges. You'll slip up. You'll second-guess yourself. That's okay. Self-love has nothing to do with being without flaws—it's about progress. Celebrate your wins, learn from your losses, and keep moving forward.

What Happens When You Value Your Standards

The moment you start valuing your standards, everything changes. You stop chasing love and start attracting it. You stop justifying bad behavior and start walking away from it. You stop settling for the life you have and start creating the life you want.

And get this: people will notice. They'll see the way you carry yourself, the way you speak, the way you refuse to settle. They'll be drawn to it, inspired by it, maybe even intimidated by it. But that's not your concern. Your concern is you—your happiness, your peace, your well-being.

Because when you value your standards, you're not just setting the tone for your relationships. You're setting the tone for your life. You're telling the world, "This is who I am. This is what I deserve. And I won't accept anything less." And that? That's power. That's freedom. That's love.

Forgiveness As Freedom

Forgiveness Is Not A Gift For Them; It's A Gift For You.

A Declaration Of Freedom

Forgiveness isn't just a choice; it's a rebellion. It's the ultimate declaration that you are no longer in the business of allowing pain to dictate your life. Think of forgiveness as slipping out of a tight dress you've outgrown—a little awkward at first, but pure relief when you're free. Forgiveness isn't about letting them off the hook—it's about setting yourself free. It's the decision to say, "I deserve peace, even if they never apologize."

And here's the kicker: forgiveness doesn't need their permission. It doesn't wait for their "I'm sorry" or their explanation. Forgiveness is for you—it's the reset button on the grip they had on your soul.

Why Forgiveness Is Essential For Healing

Anger is addictive. It whispers in your ear, promising power, but delivers exhaustion. Resentment is the faux fur coat you wear on a sweltering day—hot, heavy, and completely unnecessary. The longer you hold on to the pain, the more it defines you. And darling, you are not your scars. Forgiveness doesn't mean forgetting; it means you've decided not to let the wound fester.

Forgiveness is a quiet revolution. It's taking back the narrative. It's saying, "You hurt me, but you don't get to hold me here. I'm moving forward, with or without your remorse." Because the truth is, replaying the hurt only rewrites the story with you as the victim—and you are so much more than that.

Acknowledge Your Pain

Let's not gloss over it: they shattered you. You felt it in your chest, in your stomach, in the tears you cried until they became dry heaves. Name that pain. Write it. Shout it. Let it simmer until you're ready to pour it out. Suppressing pain is like trying to hold a beach ball underwater—it's going to pop up eventually, and not in a pretty way. Acknowledge it, because ignoring it only gives it power.

Here is a space for you to write it out.

_____

_____

_____

_____

_____

_____

_____

_____

_____

_____

_____

_____

_____

_____

_____

_____

_____

_____

_____

_____

_____

_____

_____

_____

_____

Understand Their Limitations And Letting Go Of The Need For Closure

Not everyone is capable of love. Let that sink in. Some people are emotionally tone-deaf. They can't love you the way you deserve because they don't know how. It's not an excuse for their behavior, but it is a reason to stop internalizing their inability to meet you halfway. Their shortcomings don't define your worth. It's like being mad at a chair for not being a table—pointless.

Closure is the unicorn of healing. You keep chasing it, but it doesn't exist—at least not in the way you think. You don't need their words or their explanations to close the book. Closure is a gift you give yourself. It's looking at the story and deciding, "This chapter ends here."

Forgiving Yourself For Staying Too Long

IF we're being brutally honest: you stayed because you believed. You believed in their potential, in their promises, in the fantasy that they could change. There's no shame in that. Loving someone deeply is not a flaw—it's a testament to your heart. But now it's time to forgive yourself for loving blindly, for hoping against hope, for not leaving sooner. Forgiveness starts with the mirror.

Words Of Forgiveness Towards Yourself For

- "I forgive myself for staying in a place that didn't serve me."

- "I honor the lessons I've learned and release the pain."

139

- "I am not defined by my past decisions; I am defined by my growth."

- "I choose to love myself, unconditionally and unapologetically."

Write out here what you forgive yourself for.

_____

_____

_____

_____

_____

_____

_____

_____

_____

_____

_____

_____

_____

_____

_____

_____

_____

_____

_____

Steps To Practicing Forgiveness

Forgiveness isn't a light switch; it's a dimmer. Here's how to turn it up:

Write A Letter

Put it all out there. Every ounce of anger, every "How dare you?" and "Why did you?" Let the words spill out like a confession. Don't edit yourself. And then—burn it. Shred it. Toss it into the sea. The ritual of destruction is your first act of reclaiming power.

Create A Ritual

Light a candle and breathe. Whisper to yourself, "I release this pain. I reclaim my peace." Make it a ceremony of letting go. Repeat it as often as necessary until the flame inside you feels steady again.

Start A Gratitude Practice

Shift your focus. Gratitude is like a lighthouse in a storm. It reminds you of what's good, even when the seas are rough. Write down what you've learned—about boundaries, about resilience, about yourself. Gratitude doesn't erase the hurt, but it reframes the story.

What Forgiveness Feels Like

Forgiveness feels like breathing after holding your breath for far too long. It's the weight lifting from your chest, the clarity returning to your mind. It's not an overnight transformation, but a gradual release. And one day, you wake up and realize—you're free. Not free of the memory, but free of the power it held over you.

The IT Girl's Approach To Forgiveness

An IT Girl doesn't carry grudges—they're bad for her posture. She forgives, not because they deserve it, but because she deserves peace. Forgiveness is her private weapon, her way of saying, "You don't get to live rent-free in my head."

The IT Girl knows forgiveness isn't weakness; it's strength. She doesn't confuse forgiving with forgetting. She lets go of the past because she's too busy building her future. And when she forgives, it's not a whisper; it's a roar: "I choose me."

So remember that forgiveness isn't easy, but it's necessary. It's the bridge between pain and peace, between holding on and letting go. Forgiveness is your declaration that you are more than what happened to you. It's your permission slip to thrive.

Let this chapter be your guide, your cheerleader, and your wake-up call. Choose forgiveness. Choose freedom. Choose you. Because the best revenge isn't holding on to the hurt—it's living so fully that the hurt can't touch you anymore.

What Emotional Independence Looks Like in Action
Emotional Independence: Loving Someone Without Losing Yourself

You know what no one tells you about love? It's not about searching for someone to complete you—it's the beauty of finding someone who enhances your life. But that only happens when you already stand whole on your own. Think about it: how can anyone truly love you if you keep handing them pieces of yourself, hoping they'll assemble you into something whole? You don't need fixing. You've never needed fixing. You are not a project, and love isn't a construction zone. It's an invitation to share your life, not surrender it.

Let me ask you something—how many times have you dimmed your light because you thought it might blind someone else? How many times have you silenced your voice, your needs, your desires, because you didn't want to rock the boat? Loving someone shouldn't feel like erasing parts of yourself. It should feel like adding chapters to an already epic story. And here's the truth: the right love doesn't ask for your silence; it thrives on your voice. It's time to stop whispering your needs when you're meant to roar.

The Trap We Fall Into

Have you ever woken up and realized that your life no longer feels like yours? Maybe it wasn't a sudden moment, but a slow, quiet unraveling that you barely noticed at first. You fell in love—the kind of love that sweeps you off your feet and carries you into a whirlwind of emotion. At first, it felt like magic. Their texts were the highlight of your day, their laughter a sound you wanted to wrap yourself in. You began to see your future through their eyes, adjusting your dreams to fit their plans without even realizing you were doing it.

And then, piece by piece, you started rearranging your world to fit theirs. Canceling brunches with friends because they wanted to stay in. Pushing aside hobbies that once lit up your soul because their interests took precedence. You didn't just share your life with them; you handed it over, one piece at a time, until you were left holding only fragments of the person you used to be.

But here's where it gets complicated. It wasn't that you weren't happy—at least, not entirely. The happiness was there, but it felt muted, like someone else's joy that you were borrowing. Your laughter wasn't as loud. Your dreams? They became blurry, like distant echoes of a life you once imagined but couldn't quite grasp anymore. And when you looked in the mirror, the woman staring back at you felt foreign. The spark in her eyes was dim, replaced by a quiet sadness that whispered, *Is this really all there is?*

Now let's go deeper. How many times did you convince yourself that this was love? That this sacrifice, this constant bending and reshaping of your life, was what it meant to care deeply? How long did you tell yourself that losing pieces of yourself was just the price of being loved? Because here's the truth—that's not love. Real love doesn't ask you to erase yourself. It doesn't demand that you fade into the background so someone else can take center stage. Love should feel like a duet, not a solo performance where you're just a shadow in the wings.

Here's the hardest part to admit: sometimes, we step out of the spotlight willingly. We tell ourselves, *If I'm quieter, easier, less complicated, maybe they'll stay.* We shrink, not because anyone explicitly asked us to, but because we're afraid of what will happen if we take up too much space. But shrinking yourself to make someone else comfortable isn't love; it's fear. And fear, no matter how we dress it up, is a terrible foundation for a relationship.

And if you've ever thought, *Maybe if I'm less, they'll stay longer,* let this be the moment you let that lie go. Because the truth is, you are not too much. You are not too opinionated, too ambitious, or too independent. You are exactly enough for the kind of love that doesn't diminish you but expands you. And if someone can't handle your light, that's not a reflection of your worth; it's a reflection of their limits.

This isn't just about leaving behind what no longer serves you—it's the fearless act of stepping boldly into the life you deserve. A life where your dreams aren't sacrificed, where your laughter rings loud, and where your reflection in the mirror feels like coming home. It's time to reclaim your space, your joy, and your identity. Because this is your life, and it's too beautiful to live it in anyone else's shadow. kind of love that sweeps you off your feet, intoxicating and all-consuming. At first, it was thrilling. Their texts became the highlight of your day, their laughter a melody you wanted to bottle up and keep forever. But then, without even noticing it, you started rearranging your world to fit theirs. You skipped brunch with your friends because they needed you. You let your hobbies fall by the wayside because their interests took priority. You didn't just share your life with them; you handed it over piece by piece.

And somewhere along the way, you stopped hearing your own laughter. It wasn't that you weren't happy—at least, that's what you told yourself—but the happiness felt muted, like it belonged to someone else. Your dreams? They became blurry, distant things that felt more like someone else's memories. You'd look in the mirror and see a version of yourself that felt foreign. The spark in your eyes was dimmed, the lines of your smile softened, as though the parts of you that once shined so brightly had quietly stepped aside to make room for them.

Now let me ask you this: how long did you tell yourself this was love? That this was what it meant to care deeply, to be in a partnership? How long did you convince yourself that losing pieces of yourself was just the price of being loved? Because here's the truth—that's not love. Love doesn't erase you. It doesn't ask you to fade into the background while someone else takes center stage. Love, real love, should feel like a duet, not a solo performance where you're just the backup singer.

Here's the hardest part to admit: sometimes we willingly step out of the spotlight because we're afraid of what will happen if we demand to be seen. We tell ourselves, *If I'm quieter, easier, less complicated, maybe they'll stay.* But shrinking yourself to keep someone else comfortable isn't love; it's fear. And fear is a terrible foundation for anything, let alone a relationship.

Now, let's go deeper. Have you ever told yourself, *If I'm easier to love, they'll stay?* That's the kind of lie fear tells. Fear whispers that you're too much—too opinionated, too ambitious, too independent. But fear is a terrible storyteller. Because the truth is, you're not too much. The right person will never ask you to shrink—and if they do, they're not your person. Real love doesn't diminish you; it expands you. And if someone can't handle your light, that's not your problem. It's theirs.

What Is Emotional Vulnerability?

Emotional vulnerability is the best-kept quiet ingredient in meaningful connections. It's that soft, raw space where love flourishes, where you let someone see you in all your unfiltered glory. Vulnerability done right creates bonds that feel unshakable. But when vulnerability shifts into dependency, it stops being a strength and becomes a trap. That's when emotional vulnerability starts looking less like connection and more like survival.

Dependency isn't romantic. It's exhausting. It's tying your happiness, your confidence, and even your identity to someone else's actions or approval. Love becomes a lifeline, and you're left dangling every time they pull away. Have you been there? Hanging on their words, their moods, their attention, as if your very sense of self depends on them? It's not love, my dear—it's an emotional straitjacket.

When Vulnerability Turns Toxic

Let's think about this: you're laughing off a comment that cuts deep because you don't want to "ruin the moment." You're swallowing your needs because asking for something feels like you're walking on a tightrope over their unpredictable reactions. Sound familiar? That's emotional vulnerability turned toxic.

Toxic vulnerability is trading your voice, your desires, and your boundaries for the illusion of peace. It's telling yourself that their happiness is more important than your own. It's a kind of slow erosion, where you give up little pieces of yourself one by one, thinking that's what love requires.

Let's pause. When was the last time you silenced your feelings to keep the peace? The last time you smiled through something that hurt because you didn't want to seem "difficult"? That's not vulnerability—that's self-abandonment dressed up as sacrifice. And it's time to break that cycle.

Recognizing Emotional Triggers

Here's where it gets real (again). Emotional triggers are those sneaky landmines that send you spiraling before you even realize what's happening. Maybe it's the way they casually cancel plans, making you feel like an afterthought. Or the way they dismiss your concerns with a casual, "You're too sensitive."

These moments are like little earthquakes, shaking the ground beneath you. But the tremors aren't just about what's happening now. They're tied to old wounds—an absent parent who didn't show up, an ex who chipped away at your self-worth, or a friend who only called when they needed something. Triggers don't come from nowhere. They're rooted in the stories you've been carrying.

Think about it. When was the last time someone's actions made you feel small? Like you had to shrink yourself to fit into their world? That's not love; that's emotional manipulation wrapped up in pretty packaging.

But here's the good news: your triggers aren't weaknesses. They're signals. Signals that something needs healing, that your past is asking for attention. And healing starts with awareness.

What Emotional Vulnerability Should Look Like

Healthy vulnerability is a two-way street. It's sharing your fears, your dreams, your truths, and being met with understanding, not judgment. It's letting someone see your mess without fearing they'll use it against you. Vulnerability should feel like a safe space, not a tightrope walk.

But here's the catch: you can't control how someone else reacts to your vulnerability. What you can control is who you choose to share it with. Not everyone deserves to see your unfiltered self. Vulnerability without boundaries is like leaving your front door wide open and wondering why strangers keep walking in.

How To Take Your Power Back

Reclaiming your power doesn't mean shutting people out or building walls so high no one can climb them. It means building a foundation so solid that even if someone walks away, you're still standing strong. Here's how:

1. Name Your Patterns

Start by identifying where your emotional vulnerability has turned into dependency. Did you find yourself avoiding certain conversations or simply treading lightly with them? Did you hesitate to share how you feel because you're afraid of their reaction? Write it down. The first step to change is recognizing the pattern.

Write it out below....

_____

_____

_____

_____

_____

_____

_____

_____

_____

_____

_____

_____

_____

_____

_____

_____

_____

_____

_____

_____

_____

_____

2. What Would Your Ideal Self Say

Now think of your ideal self. Who is she? What would she say and how would she act? What truths does she believe? Create her here and be her.

Write your ideal self here....

_____

_____

_____

_____

_____

_____

_____

_____

_____

_____

_____

_____

_____

_____

_____

_____

_____

_____

_____

_____

3. Set Boundaries

Boundaries aren't about keeping people out; they're about showing people how to treat you. Start small. Maybe it's saying, "I need time to process before I respond," or refusing to tolerate dismissive comments. Boundaries are your way of saying, "This is my worth, and I'm not negotiating it."

4. Reclaim Your Voice

Silence isn't golden when it costs you your peace. Speak up when something doesn't sit right. You don't have to be confrontational to be firm. Use statements like, "When you dismiss my feelings, it hurts. I need what I am saying to be approached with respect." Your voice is your power—use it.

5. Build Inner Resilience

Emotional resilience doesn't mean you'll never get hurt—it's the strength to rise and rebuild when you do. Spend time doing things that remind you who you are outside of the relationship. Pursue hobbies, connect with friends, and invest in self-care. The stronger your sense of self, the less likely you are to lose yourself in someone else.

Scenarios That Demand Your Attention

Let's break this down into real-life moments—those times when you feel your power slipping away:

1. The Dismissive Comment: Someone says something that stings and brush it off with, "I was just kidding." Your instinct might be to let it slide, but here's your moment to reclaim your power. Pause and say, "That didn't feel like a joke to me. Can we talk about it?" Addressing it sets the tone for how you deserve to be treated.

2. The Emotional Rollercoaster: They're (anyone) distant one day and overly attentive the next. Instead of chasing their highs and lows, ground yourself. Remind yourself, "Their inconsistency doesn't define my worth."

3. The Silent Treatment: They're withholding communication, and it's making you spiral. Instead of begging for their attention, focus on yourself. Use the silence to reconnect with things that bring you joy—a favorite book, a walk, or time with someone who values you.

Journaling Prompts To Heal

Self-reflection is where the magic happens. Let's dig into these questions on the next page.

What parts of myself have I silenced to maintain this relationship?

_____

_____

_____

_____

_____

_____

_____

_____

_____

_____

_____

_____

_____

_____

_____

_____

_____

_____

_____

_____

_____

_____

When was the last time I felt joy that wasn't tied to someone else's approval?

_____

_____

_____

_____

_____

_____

_____

_____

_____

_____

_____

_____

_____

_____

_____

_____

_____

_____

_____

_____

_____

_____

_____

What does love mean to me now and do I believe I was receiving it in my last relationship?

_____

_____

_____

_____

_____

_____

_____

_____

_____

_____

_____

_____

_____

_____

_____

_____

_____

_____

_____

_____

_____

_____

_____

_____

What would I tell my younger self about boundaries and self-worth?

_____

_____

_____

_____

_____

_____

_____

_____

_____

_____

_____

_____

_____

_____

_____

_____

_____

_____

_____

_____

_____

_____

_____

_____

_____

_____

How can I show myself love every day, even in small ways?

_____

_____

_____

_____

_____

_____

_____

_____

_____

_____

_____

_____

_____

_____

_____

_____

_____

_____

_____

_____

_____

_____

_____

_____

Daily Affirmations

Words shape your reality. Start each day with affirmations that remind you of your strength:

- "I am whole, worthy, and enough."

- "I release the need to seek validation from others."

- "My happiness is my responsibility."

- "I honor my boundaries and protect my peace."

- "I let go of what no longer serves me."

Now, write down the affirmations you choose to repeat to yourself daily.

_____

_____

_____

_____

_____

_____

_____

_____

_____

_____

_____

_____

_____

_____

_____

Building The Life You Deserve

Reclaiming your power isn't just about walking away from what drains you—it's the intentional choice to move toward what energizes and fulfills you. Start by asking yourself these questions:

What makes me feel most alive?

_____

_____

_____

_____

_____

_____

_____

_____

_____

_____

_____

_____

_____

_____

_____

_____

_____

_____

_____

_____

_____

_____

What relationships bring me energy instead of taking it away?

_____

_____

_____

_____

_____

_____

_____

_____

_____

_____

_____

_____

_____

_____

_____

_____

_____

_____

_____

_____

_____

_____

_____

What do I want my life to look like a year from now?

_____

_____

_____

_____

_____

_____

_____

_____

_____

_____

_____

_____

_____

_____

_____

_____

_____

_____

_____

_____

_____

_____

_____

_____

_____

_____

_____

Emotional vulnerability is not your enemy. When balanced with boundaries and self-respect, it's your superpower. But when it turns into dependency, it steals your light. Reclaiming your power starts with recognizing that your worth isn't up for negotiation. It's setting boundaries, rewriting your story, and rediscovering the parts of yourself that were never lost—just hidden.

Because here's the truth: love doesn't ask you to shrink. It asks you to grow. And the right love? It'll meet you in your fullness, not your fragments.

Learning From Your Past

We've all been there—the relationship that left you feeling invisible, where your voice grew softer and your dreams smaller because you thought that was the cost of being loved. You said yes when your heart screamed no because you believed that saying no might mean losing them. You gave so much of your time, your energy, your soul, thinking it would somehow secure the love you craved. But here's the complete truth—what you have to give isn't just yours to hand over. It's yours to protect, to treasure, and to invest in yourself first.

Think back to the woman you were in those moments. She was strong—even when she felt weak. She was brave—even when fear whispered that she wasn't enough. But she was also tired, wasn't she? Tired of giving so much and receiving so little. What did she set aside in the name of love? Her creativity, that spark that once lit up rooms? Her ambition, the dreams she whispered to herself late at night? Her boundaries, the ones she knew she needed but let slide because she thought love was more important?

Look back at her now, but do it with tenderness, not judgment. She wasn't failing; she was surviving. She did what she thought she had to do in that moment to feel worthy of love. But survival isn't the goal anymore. Thriving is. And that means taking everything she left behind—every dream deferred, every boundary ignored, every spark dimmed—and bringing it back into the light. It's never too late to reclaim what was yours all along.

Here's the beauty of your past: it's not a punishment; it's a lesson. Every time you felt small, every moment you said yes when you meant no, every time you looked in the mirror and wondered where *you* had gone—those moments weren't wasted. They were a reminder of who you never want to be again. So, look back not to dwell, but to understand. What did that version of you need most? What would have helped her stand taller, speak louder, dream bigger?

You owe it to her—to the woman who fought through the doubt and the fear—to rise now. To take her sacrifices and transform them into the foundation of the life she dreamed of but didn't yet know how to build. She gave so much to survive; now it's time to thrive. Because here's the truth: you are not behind. You are not too late. Time isn't your enemy; it's your ally. This is your life, and every moment—past, present, and future—is yours to claim. You can rewrite this story. You can become the woman she always dreamed you'd be.

Part 3:
The IT Girl Reset

The IT Girl Reset...

There's a certain power in pressing pause, a kind of rebellion against the chaos of chasing connections that leave you feeling empty. Sometimes, the most daring, unapologetic thing you can do is say, "Not right now." Not to love, not to dating, not to the never-ending pursuit of someone to complete you. Instead, you take a step back and choose yourself.

This isn't a retreat. It's a reset. A chance to rewrite the rules, to rebuild, to remind yourself who you are before anyone else tried to tell you. Because what you should know—an IT Girl doesn't date for the sake of it. She doesn't let her life orbit around someone who hasn't proven they're worth the space. She knows when it's time to close the door, sit with herself, and let the silence teach her what the noise never could.

This is the IT Girl's Relationship Reset: a detox for the heart and mind, a recalibration of standards, and the ultimate act of self-respect. Let's walk through how to reset, rebuild, and emerge with the kind of clarity and confidence that turns heads—not because you're looking for validation, but because you're glowing from the inside out.

A Step-By-Step Guide For Taking A Break From Dating

There's a certain power in pressing pause, a kind of rebellion against the chaos of chasing connections that leave you feeling empty. Sometimes, the most daring, unapologetic thing you can do is say, "Not right now." Not to love, not to dating, not to the never-ending pursuit of someone to complete you. Instead, you take a step back and choose yourself.

This isn't a retreat. It's a reset. A chance to rewrite the rules, to rebuild, to remind yourself who you are before anyone else tried to tell you. Because the reality is—an IT Girl doesn't date for the sake of it. She doesn't let her life orbit around someone who hasn't proven they're worth the space. She knows when it's time to close the door, sit with herself, and let the silence teach her what the noise never could.

This is the IT Girl's Relationship Reset: a detox for the heart and mind, a recalibration of standards, and the ultimate act of self-respect. Let's walk through how to reset, rebuild, and emerge with the kind of clarity and confidence that turns heads—not because you're looking for validation, but because you're glowing from the inside out.

Let's face it: the dating world can feel like a circus. Between swiping, texting, ghosting, and decoding mixed signals, it's no wonder so many end up emotionally drained. Taking a break isn't giving up; it's clearing the stage to create space for something better.

Step 1: Commit To The Break

Here's the first rule: you can't half-commit to a reset. This isn't about swearing off love forever—it's a conscious decision to step back and prioritize yourself. Decide how long you'll take a break (30 days, 90 days, or even six months), and stick to it. No late-night texts, no "just checking in" messages, no opening the apps for "research." Treat this time as sacred.

What To Do:
- **Delete The Apps:** Yes, all of them. Even the one where you've got "potential" matches waiting.

- **Set Boundaries:** If someone from your past tries to creep back in, politely let them know you're focusing on yourself right now.

- **Focus On You:** Remember, this isn't about running away from dating—it's the deliberate choice to run toward yourself.

Step 2: Reconnect With Yourself

Remember who you were before you started bending, compromising, and over-giving in relationships? That version of you—the one with hobbies, dreams, and a fire that didn't depend on anyone else—is still there. It's time to bring her back.

Think about the last time you lost yourself in someone else. Maybe it was the constant texting, the waiting for calls, or the way their priorities seemed to trump yours. Reconnecting with yourself is about flipping the script. It's about being so in love with your own life that anything or anyone else becomes a bonus, not the main event.

What To Do:

- **Rediscover Your Passions:** What did you love to do before the relationship? Was it painting, running, cooking, or simply binge-watching documentaries? Dive back in.

- **Create A "Me Time" Routine:** Schedule solo dates with yourself. Go to a café, take a long bath, or spend an afternoon exploring a museum.

- **Make Space For Joy:** Find the small things that light you up and do them unapologetically.

Step 3: Reflect On The Lessons

While you're taking this break, use the time to reflect deeply on what your relationships have taught you—not just about others, but about yourself. The goal isn't to linger in regret but to extract wisdom. What patterns do you keep repeating? What red flags do you now see in hindsight? And perhaps most importantly, where have you ignored your own needs to keep the peace?

What To Ask Yourself:

- "What qualities in my past partners actually brought out the best in me?"

- "Where did I confuse intensity for love or attention for care?"

- "What unmet needs did I tolerate, and why did I think I couldn't ask for more?"

- "What role did I play in the relationship dynamic? Was I over-giving, people-pleasing, or staying silent when I needed to speak up?"

- "What habits or standards do I need to implement to ensure my next relationship feels safe, reciprocal, and aligned?"

Take this time to dig into the subtle moments too—the ones you brushed off as "no big deal" but secretly chipped away at your sense of peace. Ask yourself if those compromises were worth it or if they've taught you what to no longer accept.

Here is a place to answer these questions and write down your thoughts.

_____

_____

_____

_____

_____

_____

_____

_____

_____

_____

_____

_____

_____

_____

_____

_____

_____

_____

_____

_____

_____

_____

_____

_____

_____

_____

_____

_____

_____

_____

How To Rebuild Clarity After A Breakup

Breakups can leave you feeling shattered, but they're also an opportunity. An opportunity to rebuild yourself into someone stronger, wiser, and more aligned with what you truly deserve.

Step 1: Reclaim Your Identity

After a breakup, it's easy to feel like you've lost a piece of yourself. Maybe you defined yourself through the relationship, or maybe you were so focused on being "us" that you forgot about "you." Now is the time to reclaim your identity.

You're standing in front of your closet, staring at outfits you wore because he liked them. You're scrolling through playlists, skipping songs because they remind you of him. Emotional independence begins here—when you start reclaiming those little pieces of yourself.

What To Do:

- **Purge The Past:** Donate clothes, delete playlists, and unfollow accounts that keep you tethered to the relationship.

- **Reinvent Yourself:** Get a new haircut, rearrange your living space, or pick up a new skill. Transformation is empowering.

Step 2: Shift The Narrative

A breakup doesn't mean failure. It means growth. Instead of focusing on what you lost, focus on what you gained— lessons learned, red flags spotted, and the clarity of knowing what you don't want.

What To Tell Yourself:

- "This isn't the end of my story; it's a plot twist."
- "I'm not starting over; I'm starting from experience."

Step 3: Surround Yourself With Support

Healing is hard, but you don't have to do it alone. Lean on your friends, family, or even a therapist. Surround yourself with people who remind you of your worth and reflect the kind of love you're striving for.

What To Do:

- **Create A Support System:** Reach out to friends who lift you up, not the ones who secretly enjoy your misery.

- **Set Boundaries:** If someone in your circle is making you feel worse, it's okay to take a step back.

Identifying Patterns And Creating New Habits

To break free from unhealthy relationship cycles, you have to recognize the patterns that keep you stuck. Are you drawn to emotionally unavailable people? Do you confuse intensity with love? Identifying these patterns is the first step to breaking them.

Step 1: Spot The Red Flags In Yourself

It's not just about identifying red flags in others—it's the self-awareness to recognize the ways you might sabotage your own happiness. Do you overlook red flags because you don't want to be alone? Do you compromise too quickly to keep the peace?

What To Ask Yourself:
- "What am I afraid of losing if I stay single for a while?"
- "How do I react when someone crosses a boundary?"

Step 2: Replace Old Habits With New Ones

Habits shape your reality. If your habit has been to over give, people-please, or settle, it's time to rewrite the script.

What To Do:
- **Practice Saying "No":** The next time someone asks for something that drains you, politely decline.

- **Set a Weekly "Check-In":** Reflect on whether your actions align with your values.

Step 3: Set Standards For The Future

Once you've identified the patterns you want to leave behind, it's time to create a blueprint for the love you want to build. This is where your firm boundaries come in. This is where you decide that your next relationship will feel like home—not another warzone.

What To Write Down:
- "I want a partner who communicates openly and listens actively."

- "I refuse to tolerate emotional unavailability, dishonesty, or inconsistency."

The IT Girl's Needed Reset

By the end of this reset, you'll uncover a truth that many overlook in the rush for connection: love isn't just a solution;

it's a celebration. It never about finding someone to fill the gaps in your life but someone who adds depth and meaning to the masterpiece you're already creating. The IT Girl understands this with unwavering clarity—she doesn't approach relationships as a rescue mission or a shortcut to happiness. She sees them as an enhancement to an already vibrant existence. A relationship isn't meant to overshadow who you are; it's meant to highlight your brightest parts, the way lighting enhances a diamond's sparkle.

Here's where it gets real: this reset isn't just about relationships with others—it's a reclamation of the most important relationship you'll ever have: the one with yourself. It's the moment you look at your own reflection and finally recognize the beauty, power, and potential that have always been there. It's the shedding of old narratives— the ones that insist you're only complete when you're chosen, validated, or loved by someone else. Instead, you rewrite the story: *I am the prize, the gift, the destination.*

When you approach love this way, the concept of settling becomes not just unthinkable but laughable. The IT Girl doesn't lower her standards to make someone else comfortable—she holds them high as an invitation for the right person to rise. And let's be clear: this isn't about arrogance—it's a matter of alignment. You're not seeking perfection; you're seeking reciprocity, respect, and authenticity—qualities that should be non-negotiable for anyone.

The more grounded you become in your own worth, the less you'll find yourself chasing people who were never meant for you. When you cultivate that unshakable sense of self, you create an energy that's magnetic—not because you're trying to attract anyone but because your confidence shines so brightly it becomes undeniable. The right people—the ones who see you, value you, and want to build with you—will naturally gravitate toward that light. They won't approach you to fix them or fill their voids; they'll come as whole individuals ready to create something extraordinary with you.

And here's the twist: this reset isn't just about relationships with others—it's a deep reconnection with yourself. It's the process of redefining how you see your own worth. When you become so grounded in your value, settling becomes laughable—an idea you wouldn't entertain even on your loneliest day. This isn't about being unapproachable or demanding—it's the power of standing so firmly in who you are that only those who truly respect and align with you will have the privilege of stepping into your world.

You set the bar intentionally high, creating a space where only those who truly align with your values and priorities can reach it. This isn't about exclusivity for the sake of it—it's the recognition that your standards are a direct reflection of your self-respect. The ones who rise to meet those standards do so not out of obligation or to win your approval, but because they share the same level of integrity and commitment. This creates relationships rooted in mutual understanding and genuine connection, not performative gestures or superficial compatibility.

Here's what you'll come to realize during this time: the IT Girl doesn't chase validation. She doesn't wait for someone to choose her. She chooses herself first, and in doing so, creates a magnetic energy that naturally attracts the right people. The ones who value her, respect her, and see her as she truly is—a whole, complete person.

What To Remember:
- "I don't need to rush love—it will find me when I'm ready."

- "My worth isn't determined by my relationship status."

- "Taking a break doesn't mean giving up; it means leveling up."

- "Being alone isn't a void to fill—it's a canvas to create on."

So here's the challenge: take the time. Reflect, refine, and rebuild. Because when you do, you won't just be ready for love—you'll be ready for the kind of love that feels like home. A love that doesn't ask you to shrink or compromise but to grow and expand. And isn't that the kind of love the IT Girl deserves?

The Declaration: The Glow-Up After The Storm

Heartbreak is inevitable, but staying broken? That's a choice—and not one you're going to make. If love has cracked you open, consider this your golden hour, the chance to rebuild into something more luminous, more magnetic, more you than ever before. Let's get one thing crystal clear: a breakup isn't the end of your story. It's the prologue to the best chapter yet. It's your rebirth—a moment to rediscover your power, reignite your passions, and step into the kind of life that doesn't just turn heads but makes jaws drop.

This is not based on going back to who you were before. That woman? She was wonderful, but she didn't know what she knows now. This is about becoming—becoming the IT Girl who takes every lesson, every tear, and spins it into gold. The glow-up isn't just about looking good (although, let's be honest, you'll look better than ever). It's about radiating an energy so unapologetic, so undeniably yours, that every room you enter shifts just because of your presence. This isn't a phase—it's your revolution. It's the transformation of replacing love that didn't honor you with a fierce, untouchable love for yourself—one that makes you truly unstoppable.

Turning Heartbreak Into Your Greatest Catalyst For Growth

Let's talk about the beauty of starting over—the raw, messy, breathtaking freedom that comes when the slate is wiped clean. Heartbreak is not a stop sign; it's a green light. It's the universe whispering, "Go ahead, darling. You're free now. Rewrite the story you thought you had to live." Heartbreak isn't pretty, but it's real. It strips away the illusions, the compromises, the justifications you clung to for someone who didn't deserve the light you brought into their life. And what's left? You. Bare, raw, real. And ready—not to rebuild who you were, but to create a version of yourself so incredible, even you'll stand back in awe.

Think of heartbreak like fire. Yes, it burns—but it also clears. It reduces the noise, burns away the clutter, and purifies. You're not the woman who was left or overlooked or underestimated. You're the phoenix that rose. Heartbreak doesn't define you; it refines you. It's not the thing that breaks you; it's the thing that builds you into something unshakable.

The Pain That Pushes You Forward

Heartbreak isn't just losing love. It's the loss of a dream you built with someone else. It's the plans you scribbled in your mind, the routines you wrapped your life around, the vision of a future that will never be. It's the loss of the person you thought they were. And that's devastating. But let me tell you this: the life you're mourning? It wasn't the life you were meant for. The breakup wasn't a punishment; it was the universe's way of freeing you from something that was holding you back. That's not rejection—it's redirection.

And in that pain, something magical happens. Heartbreak forces you to look in the mirror and really see yourself—not through someone else's eyes, but your own. It makes you face the fears you've avoided, the insecurities you've buried, the blind spots you didn't want to admit. And while that's uncomfortable—no, downright excruciating at times—it's necessary. Because once you confront those things, they lose their power over you. You step out sharper, clearer, and fully aware of what you deserve—and what you'll never accept again.

Here's the truth no one tells you: Heartbreak doesn't ruin you. It reveals you. It strips you down to your core, and from that place, you rebuild—stronger, wiser, and more resilient than ever before.

Remember This: Think of the woman who spent years in a relationship where she felt like a shadow of herself—always dimming her light so someone else could shine brighter. Every Sunday morning, she sat quietly through his hobbies, watching him revel in his passions while her yoga mat gathered dust in the corner. She let her voice falter during arguments, not because she didn't have something to say, but because she believed keeping the peace was more important than being heard. And then it ended. Not in a blaze of clarity but in the slow unraveling of a love that had drained her one compromise at a time.

At first, she felt lost. It was like stepping out of a dark theater into the blinding daylight—disorienting, overwhelming. But as the days passed, something shifted. She realized the space he left behind wasn't emptiness; it was opportunity. She started small. One Sunday, she unrolled that yoga mat and stretched in the sunlight that poured through her window. The next, she called her girlfriends and made brunch plans—mimosas and laughter replacing the silence she'd grown accustomed to. Her voice? Slowly but surely, it came back, bolder and clearer with every conversation. And when she walked into a room now, she no longer scanned for his approval. She moved through it as if the world was hers to take—because it was.

That breakup wasn't the end of her world; it was the beginning of her rediscovery. She didn't just get back to who she was before him. No, she became someone entirely new—

a woman who knew she was never meant to shrink. Her glow? It's the kind that doesn't just light up a room; it illuminates everything she touches. And now? Sunday mornings are hers, a sacred ritual of stretching, sipping, and living unapologetically.

What To Do:

1. **Feel It All**: Let yourself grieve. Cry until your chest aches. Scream into your pillow. Write pages of letters you'll never send. Let yourself feel every crack and crevice of the pain. Because here's the truth: bottling it up will only delay the glow-up. You have to feel it to heal it.

2. **Extract The Lessons**: This is where the magic happens. Ask yourself: What did this heartbreak teach me about myself? What patterns did I allow that I'll never repeat? What standards will I refuse to lower moving forward? These aren't just lessons; they're your blueprint.

3. **Channel The Energy**: Take that ache in your chest and turn it into fuel. Pour it into something that excites you—whether it's a passion project, a fitness goal, or the dream you've been putting off for too long. Let that heartbreak become the thing that propels you toward the life you've always deserved.

You're not just surviving this heartbreak, darling. You're transforming because of it. And when you emerge? The world won't know what hit it.

The Freedom Of Being Single

I don't know if you know this but being single is freedom in its most intoxicating form. It's not a waiting room; it's an open stage where you get to script, direct, and star in your own life. For too long, women have been told that their value is tethered to someone else's presence, that being single is a temporary state of lacking. But let's shatter that myth once and for all. Single isn't a void; it's the boldest canvas you'll ever get to paint on. This isn't about what's lost—it's the recognition of everything that's now ready to unfold.

What Freedom Really Feels Like

Freedom is waking up on a Saturday morning with no text to reply to, no plans to negotiate, and no emotional gymnastics to perform. It's sipping your coffee—or wine—in silence, knowing every second of your day belongs entirely to you. Maybe you decide to meet your girlfriends for an indulgent brunch, lingering for hours over mimosas and unfiltered laughter. Or perhaps you hop on a train to the city just because you can, wandering through streets you've never walked before, letting yourself be led by curiosity rather than compromise.

But freedom isn't just about doing—it's the liberation of unbecoming. It's the release of the invisible weight you didn't even realize you were carrying. The weight of checking your phone for texts that never come. The exhaustion of tiptoeing around someone else's moods. The quiet ache of giving more of yourself than you're getting in return. In the absence of those things, you find something extraordinary:

peace. And in that peace, you discover a kind of power you never knew you had.

Freedom is also about listening—not to the noise of the world, but to yourself. What do you want? What makes your soul light up? When you finally stop living for someone else, the answers come in whispers, and then in roars.

Let's Examine Our IT Girl Because This Speaks Volumes

She's standing in the kitchen, staring at a fridge full of leftovers from a dinner she cooked the night before. It's quiet—too quiet—but not in a peaceful way. It's the kind of silence that feels like a weight pressing on your chest. She checks her phone out of habit. Nothing. And in that moment, she realizes just how much of her energy had been spent waiting—waiting for a text, a sign, some acknowledgment that she mattered. But now? Now, there's no one to wait for.

"What do I do with myself?" she mutters under her breath, almost startled by the sound of her own voice breaking the stillness. It's a question she's been avoiding for months. For years, her time had been molded around someone else's preferences. She'd cancelled plans because he "didn't feel like going out," adjusted her schedule so it matched his, and bit her tongue during arguments just to avoid rocking the boat. And now, with all the time in the world suddenly her own, she didn't know where to begin.

That's when her best friend called. "Get dressed," the voice on the other end demanded. "I'm picking you up in 20 minutes."

"I'm not really in the mood," she replied, pulling at the frayed edges of her oversized sweatshirt.

"I don't care. You don't need a mood, you need a mimosa. Be ready."

And just like that, she found herself seated at a sunlit patio table, surrounded by laughter and clinking glasses. Her best friend leaned in and said, "You're allowed to start over. You don't have to fix anything, and you don't have to figure it all out today. Just be here."

The words landed like a permission slip. For the first time in months, she didn't feel the need to explain herself or shrink into the shadows. Instead, she laughed—a real laugh, the kind that spills out before you can catch it. And in that moment, something shifted. She realized the silence back in her kitchen wasn't emptiness; it was possibility.

That week, she signed up for a painting class she'd always talked about but never pursued. She started walking to her favorite coffee shop every morning, just because she loved the way the sunlight hit the street at that hour. She didn't fill the space he left behind with distractions. She filled it with herself—her dreams, her joys, her rediscovered passions.

By the time she walked into her next meeting with her head held high and a bold red lip that screamed confidence, no one had to ask her what changed. It was written all over her. She wasn't trying to be noticed anymore. She was finally seeing herself.

What To Do:

1. **Reclaim Your Time**: Make a list of every dream, every hobby, every adventure you put on hold. Start small: a cooking class you always wanted to try, an afternoon spent painting. Then build from there.

2. **Redefine Adventure**: Book that solo trip you were too afraid to take. Wander through a bookstore with no agenda. Rediscover what makes you feel alive.

3. **Celebrate Yourself**: Don't wait for someone else to show you love—show it to yourself. Buy the flowers you love. Pop open the champagne on a random Tuesday. Write your own love story, and let it start with you.

Freedom isn't a placeholder; it's the main event. The single life isn't about passing time until someone else comes along—it's the art of claiming that space and making it so vibrant, so full, so undeniably yours that when someone does arrive, they'll have to rise to meet you. Because you? You'll be unstoppable.

Use this space to make a list of your dreams, hobbies and adventures that you have put on hold that you will actually start doing for yourself.

_____
_____
_____
_____
_____
_____
_____
_____
_____
_____
_____
_____
_____
_____
_____
_____
_____
_____
_____
_____
_____
_____
_____
_____
_____

The IT Girl Glow-Up

The glow-up isn't about revenge—it's a rebirth. It's the transformation into the kind of woman who doesn't just enter a room—she owns it. The glow-up isn't a makeover; it's a reclamation of everything you are and everything you're becoming. Sure, the external touches matter (who doesn't feel unstoppable after a fresh haircut or a new pair of heels?), but what truly sets this transformation apart is the shift that happens inside. This is about rewriting your story and showing the world—and yourself—that heartbreak didn't break you. It molded you into a masterpiece.

You know what makes this glow-up so electric? It's the way it balances the external and internal. You'll walk into every room with the confidence of someone who has nothing to prove and everything to enjoy. It's the energy of knowing that every scar, every tear, every sleepless night wasn't just endured; it was alchemized into something golden. The IT Girl glow-up isn't about proving you've moved on—it's the undeniable reminder to yourself that you're unstoppable, unshakable, and more alive than ever before.

What The Glow-Up Looks Like:
- **Appearance:** This isn't about changing yourself—it's about elevating what already makes you incredible. Maybe it's a new haircut, a skincare routine that makes you glow, or finally rocking that bold lipstick. It's the art of expressing yourself outwardly in a way that reflects the confident, radiant woman you're becoming. Imagine stepping into a boutique and trying on that dress you've always admired from

afar—only this time, you're not hesitating. You're claiming it as your own.

- **Knowledge:** The IT Girl is always growing. Read the books, take the course, learn the skill. Elevate your mind as much as your look. Intelligence is as much a part of the glow-up as a flawless complexion. Picture a quiet evening spent devouring a book about something you've always been curious about—not because you have to, but because you want to. Knowledge is the ultimate accessory.

- **Financial Power:** Heartbreak can be expensive, but your glow-up? It's an investment. Save more. Earn more. Build the kind of financial independence that feels like freedom. Start planning for your future on your terms—whether that's launching a side hustle, opening a savings account just for travel, or finally asking for that raise you know you deserve. Financial power isn't just practical; it's liberating.

- **Energy:** Walk into every room as if the past didn't shatter you but polished you. People will notice, and they'll wonder how you did it. That's the IT Girl magic It's the embodiment of an energy so magnetic that your presence speaks louder than words. It's the quiet confidence of walking with your head high— not out of arrogance, but because you've done the work, and it shows.

Let's Look At Our IT Girl (YOU)

She sat in front of her vanity mirror, the soft glow of the lights framing her reflection. Her favorite red lipstick sat untouched, a shade she hadn't worn in years because he once said it was "too much." Tonight, she picked it up, twisting the tube until the bold, vibrant color emerged. As she swept it across her lips, she felt a rush of confidence she hadn't felt in ages—a reminder of the woman she used to be before she started dimming her light.

Her phone buzzed with a message from her best friend: *"Drinks at 8. Don't be late."* She glanced at the clock. There was no hesitation, no second-guessing. She slipped on the black dress she'd been saving for a "special occasion" and looked at herself again in the mirror. This wasn't just a night out. This was a declaration: *I'm back.*

As she walked into the bar, heads turned. Not because of the dress or the lipstick, but because of the way she carried herself. She wasn't looking for validation. She was glowing with the kind of energy that says, "I don't need anyone to tell me I'm enough. I know it."

Five External Glow-Up Suggestions:
1. **Hair Transformation:** Whether it's a bold chop, subtle highlights, or a complete color switch, a hair transformation can symbolize shedding the past and stepping into your new era. Think of it as more than a haircut—it's a ritual of renewal.

2. **Wardrobe Overhaul:** Upgrade your closet with pieces that make you feel powerful and unstoppable. Think tailored blazers, statement shoes, or a dress that hugs you in all the right places. Your wardrobe should reflect who you are becoming, not who you used to be.

3. **Skincare Glow:** Invest in a skincare routine that leaves you radiant. A glowing complexion is more than vanity—it's self-care that shows on your face. Every serum and mask is an act of love for yourself.

4. **Fitness Routine:** Find a physical activity that empowers you. Whether it's pilates, running, or dance classes, moving your body is a form of reclaiming it. Each drop of sweat is proof that you're taking control.

5. **Signature Fragrance:** Find a scent that feels like you—something that lingers after you leave the room, making you unforgettable. A fragrance isn't just a scent; it's an identity.

Five Internal Glow-Up Suggestions:

1. **Set Emotional Boundaries:** Decide what you will and won't tolerate moving forward. This is your time to protect your peace unapologetically. Boundaries aren't walls; they're the rules of engagement for how you deserve to be treated. (I had to tell you this again BECAUSE IT'S IMPORTANT)

2. **Curate Your Mindset:** Replace negative self-talk with affirmations that remind you of your worth. Speak to yourself like you would a best friend. If you wouldn't say it to her, don't say it to yourself.

3. **Pursue Knowledge:** Dive into topics that intrigue you—psychology, art, personal finance, or even a language. Expanding your mind is the ultimate flex and one that never goes out of style.

4. **Cultivate Gratitude:** Start each day by listing three things you're grateful for. It's a simple act that shifts your focus to abundance instead of lack. Gratitude is the antidote to bitterness.

5. **Rediscover Joy:** Do something purely because it brings you happiness. Whether it's singing loudly in the shower, painting, or baking, find your spark and fan it. Joy is an act of rebellion against heartbreak.

What To Do:

1. **Set Higher Standards**: Write down your non-negotiables and hold yourself to them. This is your new baseline—don't settle for anything less.

2. **Upgrade Your Routine**: Start treating your life like it's a luxury experience. Light the candles, wear the good perfume, and make every day feel special.

3. **Step Into The Next Chapter**: Whatever that looks like for you, own it. Dress for it. Speak as if you're already living it. Because you are.

This Is Your Glow-Up Era

This isn't just about getting over someone—it's the rediscovery of the woman who's been patiently waiting for her turn to shine—and finally giving her the stage. The IT Girl glow-up isn't about erasing the past—it's the transformation of every lesson, every heartbreak, into the fuel that ignites your next chapter. It's the moment you look in the mirror with unshakable confidence and say, *"She didn't break me. She made me stronger, sharper, and unstoppable."*

Think of this as your rebirth. You're no longer just surviving—you're thriving. This is the moment you take everything you've learned from the heartbreak, every tear you've cried, and you use it to build a version of yourself so extraordinary, even you'll marvel at how far you've come. Because here's the truth: the glow-up isn't about reaching a final destination—it's the evolution of becoming everything you've ever dreamed of. And along the way? You'll claim the life that was always meant for you.

So here's your challenge: don't just get through this heartbreak—rise from it. Let it sharpen you, inspire you, and set you on fire in the best possible way. This is your time to rise, to shine, and to own every single part of your glow-up era. Are you ready

Part 4:
A New Approach
To Relationships

The Declaration: The IT Girl Knows Her Worth

Here's another truth that needs to be said (I know, so many truths), loud and clear: **you are the prize.** Let that settle into your bones. Too many of us have spent years auditioning for roles in love stories that were never written for us. We've twisted ourselves into shapes that felt unnatural, lowered our standards to meet someone's mediocrity, and convinced ourselves that being chosen was the ultimate win. But the IT Girl knows better. She doesn't beg for love; she commands it. She doesn't chase validation; she radiates it. She doesn't settle; she elevates. And now, it's time for you to step into that energy.

This isn't about arrogance—it's about alignment. The IT Girl knows her worth, not because someone handed it to her, but because she claimed it for herself. She's done with the narrative that love is something to suffer through. For her, love isn't a battlefield—it's a sanctuary. This chapter isn't about searching for someone to complete you—it's the realization that you were already whole. It's the kind of self-assurance that makes love an addition, not a necessity.

What Is Good Love?

Let's dismantle a myth: love is not something you earn by being smaller, quieter, or more agreeable. Real love doesn't ask you to dim your light or lower your standards. Real love meets you where you are, in all your brilliance, and says, "Let's grow together."

So why do we settle? Because society has sold us a version of love that's built on struggle. We've been told that good love is hard love, that compromise is synonymous with sacrifice, and that it's noble to endure. But the IT Girl rejects this narrative. She knows that love isn't meant to deplete her; it's meant to enrich her. And when love stops adding value, she's not afraid to walk away.

Before we get into anything we need to make this everything....

This Is Our IT Girl Anthem...

I Am

I am the woman who refuses to be defined by anyone's expectations but my own. I am the storm and the calm, the question and the answer. I am every heartbreak I survived, every dream I refused to give up, and every boundary I built to protect the woman I am becoming. I am unshakable, not because life has been easy, but because I've learned to stand tall through every moment that tried to break me. I am not waiting to be chosen—I have already chosen myself.

I Feel

I feel the ache of my worth in my bones, the kind of knowing that cannot be undone. I feel the depth of my pain, but I no longer fear it—it has only made me more alive. I feel the quiet strength that comes from walking away from what doesn't honor me and the wild joy that comes from embracing what does. I feel love, not because someone gives it to me, but because I pour it into myself daily. I feel unstoppable, even when I doubt, even when I falter, because I know that my feelings are valid, my journey is sacred, and my heart is mine to heal.

I Believe

I believe that I deserve love that doesn't make me beg. I believe in the kind of peace that doesn't come at the cost of my soul. I believe in my right to take up space, to demand more, to say "no" without guilt and "yes" without fear. I believe that every time I honor myself, I rewrite a legacy of women who were taught to settle. I believe that I am worthy—not because of what I've accomplished, but because of who I am when no one else is watching.

I Know

I know that I am the IT Girl because I have decided that I am. I know that my worth isn't measured by someone else's opinion, but by how fiercely I honor my own. I know that love—real love—starts within me, and I refuse to settle for anything that feels like less. I know that I am rare, irreplaceable, and extraordinary, not because the world tells me so, but because I choose to live like I am. And I know, without a shadow of a doubt, that the life I am creating will be as bold, beautiful, and unapologetically mine as I am.

Now let's get back to this.

Characteristics Of An IT Girl's Love

Here's what love looks like for the woman who knows her worth:

1. Mutual Respect

The IT Girl doesn't settle for being tolerated; she demands to be celebrated. In her love story, respect is non-negotiable. Her opinions aren't dismissed; they're valued. Her boundaries aren't tested; they're honored. Mutual respect isn't just a nice-to-have; it's the foundation.

Respect goes beyond manners; it's in the details. It's how they listen to your dreams without interrupting. It's the way they respect your time, your space, and your individuality. Love without respect is not love—it's obligation dressed up as affection.

2. Emotional Safety

She knows that vulnerability without safety is a recipe for heartache. Emotional safety means she can show up as her full, authentic self—tears, fears, and all—without fear of judgment. Her emotions are met with compassion, not condescension.

True emotional safety feels like being seen and still being accepted. It's knowing that you can voice your concerns without walking on eggshells. For the IT Girl, emotional safety is non-negotiable. She won't shrink her feelings to protect someone else's ego.

3. Consistency

The IT Girl has no time for emotional whiplash. She's not interested in hot-and-cold, come-and-go love. For her, consistency is sexy. It's showing up, following through, and matching actions with words.

Consistency isn't boring; it's stabilizing. It's texting back when you say you will. It's planning dates instead of making excuses. It's being predictable in the best way—not because you're a routine, but because you're reliable. For the IT Girl, consistency is what separates love from lust.

4. Support For Growth

Her love isn't a cage; it's a catalyst. She's with someone who cheers for her wins, celebrates her ambitions, and isn't intimidated by her glow-up. Love, for her, is a partnership where both people are committed to evolving.

Growth doesn't mean perfection; it means progression. The right partner doesn't hold you back—they push you forward. They're not just present for the good days; they're invested in your growth during the hard ones.

Understanding What Real Love Looks Like

Let's Paint A Picture Of Love That Feels Like Home.

Defining Real Love

Love isn't meant to be a guessing game or a marathon of emotional endurance. Real love is steady, intentional, and grounding. It's not the whirlwind that sweeps you off your feet only to leave you in freefall—it's the steady anchor that holds you during life's storms.

Real love feels like peace. It's not flashy or chaotic; it's consistent. It's showing up every single day, in big and small ways. It's the text that says, "I'm thinking of you" when they know you've had a long day. It's the quiet comfort of their presence when words aren't needed. It's being able to be your full, unfiltered self—messy, emotional, and imperfect—without fear of rejection.

Real love is a space where you can exhale. It's not a competition, nor is it a performance. It's a partnership rooted in mutual respect, trust, and unwavering support. But to truly understand what real love looks like, we must first unlearn the myths that have been sold to us about what love is supposed to be.

Characteristics Of A Healthy, Fulfilling Relationship

Here's what love should look like when it's real, healthy, and fulfilling:

Mutual Respect

Respect is the cornerstone of any great relationship. In real love, you don't have to fight for your opinions to be heard. Your partner values your thoughts as much as their own. They don't just listen; they hear you. And they're willing to grow with you, even when your perspectives differ.

Consistency

Real love is reliable. It's not a guessing game or an emotional rollercoaster. Their actions match their words. No mixed signals, no emotional whiplash—just steady commitment. Consistency doesn't mean being without mistakes; it means putting in the effort. It means showing up, even when it's hard.

Emotional Safety

You feel free to express yourself without fear of judgment or retaliation. Real love creates a safe space where you can be vulnerable without feeling exposed. It's where your emotions are welcomed, not dismissed or belittled.

Support For Growth

Real love doesn't hold you back; it propels you forward. It's cheering for your dreams, even when they challenge the status quo of the relationship. It's understanding that personal growth and love can coexist—that one doesn't have to come at the expense of the other.

How Real Love Makes You Feel Valued And Respected

It's the little things that speak volumes. It's the way they remember how you take your coffee or the song that lifts your spirits. It's the way they hold space for your tears without rushing to fix them, or how they show up for your wins without making it about them. Real love doesn't compete with you; it collaborates.

Real love makes you feel seen. It makes you feel like your thoughts, emotions, and experiences matter. It's the way they lean in during a tough conversation instead of shutting down. It's the way they're willing to admit when they're wrong, and how they're just as invested in your happiness as they are in their own.

Steps To Redefine Your Standards

If your experiences with love have left you settling for less than you deserve, it's time to raise the bar. Redefining your standards does not revolve around building walls—it's the act of elevating the foundation you stand on. Here's how to start:

Create A Love Vision Board

Visualize the relationship you want. Write down the qualities, values, and feelings you want to experience. Be unapologetically specific. Do you want a partner who communicates openly? Someone who shares your sense of adventure? Someone who makes you feel safe? Put it all on your vision board and refer to it often.

Set Non-Negotiables
What are your dealbreakers? Whether it's emotional unavailability, dishonesty, or lack of ambition, name them and stick to them. Non-negotiables aren't about being picky; they're about protecting your peace.

Learn From The Past
Reflect on your past relationships without judgment. What worked? What didn't? Use those lessons to refine your understanding of what you want. Every experience, even the painful ones, has something to teach you. The key is to let it inform your future without letting it define you.

Real Love vs. The Illusion Of Love
Let's talk about the illusion of love—the kind that's all sparks and no substance. It's intoxicating at first, but it's not sustainable. The illusion of love is rooted in infatuation, not connection. It's the whirlwind romance that burns bright but fizzles fast. Real love, on the other hand, is steady. It's built on a foundation of trust and mutual respect. It's not defined by grand gestures—it's the consistency of showing up every day, in both big and small ways.

Let's Get Clear.
Self-reflection is a powerful tool for redefining your standards. Answer this prompt to gain clarity:

"What does love mean to me, and how do I want to experience it?"

Daily Affirmations For A Love That Aligns
Affirmations can help you align your mindset with the love you want to attract. Try these:

- "I deserve a love that feels like peace."

- "I am worthy of a partner who values and respects me."

- "I let go of relationships that no longer serve me."

- "I attract love that is steady, intentional, and fulfilling."

- "I am open to a partnership that supports my growth and happiness."

Understanding what real love looks like is the first step toward experiencing it. Real love has nothing to do with perfection—it's built on partnership. It's the commitment of two people showing up for each other, day after day, with kindness, respect, and intention.

Because real love doesn't just happen—it's built. And the foundation? That's you.

Because the best love story you'll ever write starts with the relationship you have with yourself.

The Power Of Standards

Now, let's talk about standards—not preferences, not nice-to-haves, but standards. The IT Girl knows her deal breakers, and she doesn't apologize for them. Standards aren't about being high-maintenance; they're about being self-respecting. Here's how she defines hers:

Define Your Non-Negotiables

What are your dealbreakers? Dishonesty? Emotional unavailability? Lack of ambition? Write them down. Make them clear. These aren't meant to scare people off; they're meant to filter out the ones who don't align.

Non-negotiables are the pillars of your emotional well-being. They're not arbitrary—they're rooted in your values. The IT Girl knows that compromising on her dealbreakers is like building a house on a shaky foundation.

I know you wrote down your non-negotiables pages ago but after doing some more reading and thinking this is your space to include some more non-negotiables.

_____
_____
_____
_____
_____
_____
_____
_____
_____
_____
_____
_____
_____
_____
_____
_____
_____
_____

Honor Your Boundaries

Boundaries aren't walls; they're guidelines for how you expect to be treated. The IT Girl knows that boundaries aren't selfish; they're self-preserving. And if someone can't respect them, they're showing you they're not ready for the kind of love you're offering.

Boundaries aren't about keeping people out; they're about keeping your peace intact. They're the way you protect your energy, your time, and your heart. The IT Girl isn't afraid to say no because she knows that "no" to the wrong thing is a "yes" to herself.

Write out here what boundaries you will put in place and stick by.

_____

_____

_____

_____

_____

_____

_____

_____

_____

_____

_____

_____

_____

_____

_____

The IT Girl's Love Affirmations

Words are powerful, and the IT Girl knows the importance of speaking her reality into existence. Here are her love affirmations:

- "I am worthy of a love that feels like peace."
- "I attract a partner who respects and uplifts me."
- "I release the need to settle for less than I deserve."
- "My standards are a reflection of my self-respect."
- "I am complete and whole, with or without a partner."

Affirmations aren't just words; they're declarations of intention. The IT Girl repeats them until they sink into her subconscious, becoming the foundation of her self-worth.

The Work Of Becoming The IT Girl

Being the IT Girl doesn't revolve around being without imperfections—it's the power of being fully present. It means showing up for yourself in ways that make you proud. Here's how she gets there:

Build An Unshakable Sense Of Self

The IT Girl doesn't look to others to define her worth. She knows who she is, what she brings to the table, and what she deserves. This confidence isn't born overnight; it's built through self-reflection, self-care, and self-love.

An unshakable sense of self means knowing your worth even when someone else doesn't see it. It's walking away from the table when love is no longer being served.

Invest In Your Joy

Happiness isn't a destination; it's a practice. The IT Girl prioritizes activities, relationships, and habits that bring her joy. She doesn't wait for a partner to make her happy—she creates her own happiness.

Joy is an act of rebellion in a world that profits from your insecurities. The IT Girl invests in herself, knowing that happiness is the best revenge.

Radiate Authenticity

There's nothing more attractive than a woman who knows herself and isn't afraid to show it. The IT Girl doesn't wear masks to be loved. She's unapologetically authentic, and that's her superpower.

Authenticity is not tied to being flawless; it's about being real. The IT Girl knows that true connection happens when she shows up as her unfiltered self.

Releasing The Need To Be Chosen

Here's a profound shift: stop trying to be chosen and start choosing yourself. Too often, we're waiting for someone to validate us, to pick us, to say we're enough. But the IT Girl knows that her value isn't dependent on external validation. She's not looking for a seat at someone else's table—she's building her own.

Let go of the need to prove your worth. You are not an option; you are the prize. The right person won't need convincing. They'll see your worth because they'll recognize it as equal to their own.

What Love Feels Like When You Know Your Worth

Love, when it aligns with your worth, feels expansive. It doesn't shrink you; it stretches you in the best way. It's the partner who asks how your day was and genuinely listens. It's the consistency in their actions that makes you feel secure. It's the way they celebrate your wins without feeling threatened. This love doesn't ask you to choose between your dreams and your relationship—it nurtures both.

When you know your worth, love feels like freedom. Freedom to be yourself, to express yourself, to grow into the fullest version of you. It's the love that doesn't complete you but complements you.

The IT Girl doesn't wait for love to define her; she defines herself. She knows her worth and isn't afraid to walk away from anything that doesn't align with it. This chapter is your invitation to step into that energy. Stop shrinking, stop settling, and start showing up as the woman you were always meant to be.

Because here's the truth: you are the prize. And the right love? It won't need to be chased. It will meet you where you are—radiant, whole, and unapologetically you.

Her Outlook On Relationships

Let's talk about relationships—the IT Girl way. An IT Girl never begs, never chases, and never shrinks herself to fit into a story that was never hers to begin with. She's the woman who walks into a room and commands attention, not because she's trying, but because she simply *is*. And when it comes to love? She understands one crucial thing: relationships are not a measure of her worth but an extension of it.

Being this kind of woman doesn't just happen. It takes work. Emotional independence isn't something you wake up with; it's something you build, brick by brick. Discernment isn't learned overnight. And self-worth? That's the foundation that holds it all together—a foundation that won't crack under pressure, no matter how tempting the distraction or how alluring the chaos.

Here's what the IT Girl knows: she doesn't need to prove her value to anyone. She doesn't audition for the role of "worthy of love" in someone else's life. She casts herself as the lead in her own. If someone wants a supporting role, they'd better bring something to the table that complements her, not diminishes her. She knows the difference between a partnership that elevates and one that pulls her down—and she's not afraid to walk away when it's the latter.

But lets it all out. The world doesn't make it easy to stay in this mindset. You're bombarded with messages that tell you to settle—subtly, sneakily, almost as if the people pushing the narrative hope you don't notice. *Maybe you're being too picky. Maybe it's not so bad. Maybe this is as good as it gets.* These aren't just whispers from well-meaning friends or family; they're ingrained in the culture that says a relationship, any relationship, is better than none.

But you know better. You know that a relationship that drains you, diminishes you, or demands you to change the core of who you are is no relationship at all. It's a cage disguised as comfort. And you're not the kind of woman who settles for the appearance of love when you deserve the real thing.

Let's break it down. The IT Girl approach to relationships isn't wrapped up in being demanding—it's grounded in discernment. It means recognizing that love should elevate you, not diminish you. It's the certainty that the right person won't make you question your worth—they'll affirm it. Real love isn't a constant negotiation—it's a natural alignment that feels effortless, mutual, and steady.

This kind of love doesn't come from lowering your standards or compromising your values. It comes from holding firm, even when it feels lonely. And let's be real: there will be lonely moments. There will be nights when you're staring at your phone, wondering why someone hasn't called. There will be family gatherings where the dreaded question comes up: "Why are you still single?" And there will be times when it feels like everyone else is moving forward while you're stuck waiting for something more. But those moments? They're temporary. The peace that comes from not settling? That's permanent.

The IT Girl understands that relationships are not about filling a void. They're about building something extraordinary. She doesn't rationalize red flags or make excuses for bad behavior. She doesn't convince herself that "nice enough" is good enough. She knows that respect, effort, and emotional availability are non-negotiables. And she's willing to walk away when those things aren't on the table.

So, what does this look like in practice? It looks like saying no to the guy who only texts after midnight. It looks like walking away from someone who makes you feel like a second option. It looks like refusing to entertain someone who says they "don't believe in labels" when what you want is a committed relationship. And it looks like doing all of this without guilt, without apology, and without second-guessing yourself.

The IT Girl knows her worth isn't tied to someone's ability to see it. She doesn't try to convince anyone to love her. She doesn't wait for someone to "get it." She knows that the right person won't need convincing. They'll show up fully, just as she does, because they recognize the value of being with someone who knows exactly who she is.

And this isn't just about romantic relationships. The IT Girl approach applies to everything. It's the unwavering refusal to compromise your peace, your joy, or your self-respect for anything that doesn't align with your highest self. It's cultivating friendships that feel reciprocal, pursuing careers that honor your talents, and creating a life that feels full—not just fine.

So, stop worrying about being "too much" or "too selective." The right people won't see your standards as a challenge; they'll see them as a guide. They'll step up because they want to, not because you forced them to. And when they do? You'll know it's real because you didn't have to lose yourself to get there.

Because here's the little detail: when you live by your standards, you don't just attract what's good—you attract what's great. And isn't that what you deserve? Not someone who tolerates you, but someone who celebrates you. Not a relationship that feels like work, but one that feels like home. Not a life that's just okay, but one that's extraordinary.

The IT Girl knows that her standards aren't walls; they're invitations. Invitations for the right people, the right opportunities, and the right love to step forward. And when they do? She's ready, not because she lowered her standards, but because she held them high.

A Love Letter To Yourself

Let's flip the script. No, actually—let's rip it up and start fresh. What if every morning you woke up knowing, not hoping, but *knowing* that you are enough? Enough without the accolades, without the validation, without anyone's approval. Imagine living a life so unapologetically full that love isn't the centerpiece—it's the accent, the glow that enhances what's already stunning.

What if you stopped waiting? Waiting for the right moment, the right person, the right anything. What if instead, you decided that your time is *now*? Maybe it means finally blocking out the noise and reclaiming your evenings for that novel you've promised yourself for years. Maybe it's finally booking that solo trip that scares you as much as it excites you. Maybe it's choosing to stop apologizing for the times you need to put yourself first. And here's the truth: you don't need permission to do any of it. You never did.

What would that look like? Picture yourself stepping into a life where every decision—big or small—is rooted in what makes your heart beat faster. Where you stop asking if you're too much and start asking if the people around you are even enough to keep up. Because here's the untold truth: when you pour into yourself with intention and love, you stop seeking external validation. You become the kind of woman whose presence is a gift, not because you need anyone to notice, but because *you* notice.

So, ask yourself: What's been holding you back? Fear? Guilt? The false belief that your worth is tied to how much you give to everyone else? Whatever it is, let it go. Because the life you deserve—the one where you love yourself so fiercely that everything else becomes secondary—it's waiting for you. But it'll only wait so long. Choose yourself now. Because if you wait for the world to tell you you're enough, you'll be waiting forever.

The IT Girl Declaration

Let me leave you with this: the IT Girl mindset has nothing to do with being flawless—it's the courage to be unapologetically bold. It's walking away from anything that makes you feel small and stepping into everything that makes you feel limitless. It's knowing that the right kind of love doesn't ask you to give yourself away; it invites you to be more of who you already are.

So, I'll ask you again: who are you when no one's watching? Who are you when you're not trying to be loved? Because that woman—she's the one who deserves to be adored, cherished, and celebrated. And she doesn't settle for anything less than the kind of love that makes her feel like the sun.

Darling, you don't just deserve love. You deserve a love that feels like coming home—to yourself.

The IT Girl Mindset

The IT Girl doesn't barter her dreams for someone else's comfort. She doesn't contort herself into shapes to fit someone's expectations. She loves, yes, but her love doesn't come with the condition that she must lose herself to keep it alive. Emotional independence isn't just her superpower—it's her shield, her compass, her anchor. It's the silent strength that allows her to walk into a room, not with a need to be seen, but with a presence that can't help but be noticed.

The IT Girl's love is not a safety net, but a compass rose. It doesn't shelter or shield; it guides with quiet certainty. Her love provides direction without imposing control, offering clarity even in the foggiest of moments. Her love inspires, it elevates, but it never rescues—because she knows that true connection has nothing to do with being someone's savior. It's the foundation of partnership, built on equality. She's the woman who says, "I love you, but I will never lose myself to love you," and those aren't just words. They're a promise—to herself, first and foremost. Her love is a gift, not a lifeline, and that's what makes it extraordinary.

In relationships, she doesn't merely survive—she thrives. Why? Because she has learned the sacred truth that loving someone deeply and loving herself fiercely are not opposing forces. They are partners in the same dance. The IT Girl knows that the foundation of any lasting love isn't sacrifice— it's symmetry. She's not afraid to walk away from anything that asks her to shrink, because she knows she's already whole. She doesn't need someone to complete her; she's already a masterpiece.

Being the IT Girl is not centered on invincibility—it's the strength of resilience. She's not unbreakable, but she's unshakable. She's felt the sting of heartbreak, the ache of loss, and the weight of self-doubt. But she's also learned how to rebuild herself, stronger and more luminous each time. She's not afraid of losing someone, because she's made peace with the most important truth of all: she'll never lose herself. And that, my love, is where her power lies.

Building Your Future

Now, let's talk about the woman you're becoming. She's unapologetic in ways that make people stop and take notice. She doesn't flinch when it's time to say no because she knows that every no to something unworthy is a yes to herself. She's the kind of woman who can look at someone she loves, hold their gaze with calm certainty, and say, "This is what I need," not as a request, but as a truth. When someone tries to dim her light, she doesn't just shine brighter—she becomes a beacon, unyielding and undeniable.

Her love isn't fragile or timid. It's bold, deliberate, and rare. She doesn't pour it into leaky vessels or offer it as a token to anyone who merely asks. She gives it to those who prove they can hold it with care—not because she's testing them, but because she values it too much to see it wasted. She's learned that love isn't built on scarcity or games—it's a reflection of worth, and she refuses to forget hers.

This woman walks away from what doesn't serve her, but don't mistake that for ease. It takes strength to release something she once wanted, to let go of a vision she once clung to. Yet she does it, not because it's easy, but because it's necessary. Because she understands that staying in spaces that demand her to shrink will never allow her to grow. And growth, my dear, is her mission.

Here's what she knows: The moment you fully grasp your worth, you change the way the world treats you. You stop apologizing for your standards because you understand that they're not walls—they're gates, and only those who are ready to match your energy get to walk through.

Let me give you something sacred to do: tonight, find a quiet space and close your eyes. See yourself not as you are, but as the woman you're becoming. Picture her standing tall, radiating confidence and grace. Feel her energy. Let it fill the room, let it fill *you*. Meditate on her strength, her clarity, her power. Ask yourself, *What choices does she make? What does she let go of? What does she claim as her own?* When you open your eyes, write one thing she would do tomorrow—and then do it. Just one step, and then another.

Darling, the woman you're becoming isn't waiting for permission. She doesn't live by rules that others set for her. She's limitless, and so are you. This is your life, and it doesn't run on anyone else's timeline. You're not behind. You're not late. You are exactly where you're meant to be, and the future is yours to claim.

The Secret No One Talks About

The strongest love isn't defined by holding on tightly—it's the freedom of holding on with trust, knowing that what's meant for you will always stay. Emotional independence is knowing that you can love someone deeply and still love yourself more. It's the understanding that your happiness is not someone else's responsibility—it's yours.

So, here's the real question: Are you ready to choose yourself? Not in the way that pushes people away, but in the way that sets the standard for how they treat you? Because the IT Girl doesn't just survive love—she thrives in it. She makes her rules, she writes her story, and she knows, without a doubt, that she is enough.

And darling, so are you.

The Art Of Discernment: Recognizing Potential vs. Compatibility

Let's get something straight: potential is not compatibility. Potential is that shimmering mirage in the distance, the illusion we chase when reality feels like it's coming up short. It's the idea of someone becoming the partner we want them to be, not the truth of who they are. Compatibility, on the other hand, is what's tangible. It's the present. It's shared values, mutual respect, and emotional availability. It's the foundation for something real and enduring, not a gamble on what might one day exist.

Let's me be brutally honest. How many times have you found yourself defending someone's bad behavior because you believed in their "potential"? He's emotionally unavailable now, but maybe it's just stress. He doesn't prioritize you, but surely that will change once his life settles down. This trap is as common as it is dangerous. Potential offers you a reason to stay, a glimmer of hope to cling to when the present doesn't feel like enough. But here's the hard truth: you can't build a life on a foundation of maybes.

What makes potential so seductive is that it lets us believe we're investing in a future payoff. But relationships aren't about waiting for someone to evolve into who you need. They're about being with someone who's already aligned with you. Someone who doesn't require endless justifications or excuses. Compatibility is rooted in the now—in shared goals, in ease, in the way they make you feel seen and valued, not the promise of something better around the corner.

The High-Stakes Scenario: When Potential Deceives

Think back to the last time you were tangled in a relationship where potential was your compass. He wasn't present, not really. Conversations felt like a game of tug-of-war—you pulling, him barely holding the other end. Plans were never concrete, always a hazy "maybe" or "we'll see," and yet you found yourself defending him to friends who had long since spotted the cracks. You saw those cracks too, didn't you? But you convinced yourself they weren't deal breakers, just temporary flaws that love could smooth over.

So, you waited. You waited for him to text first, to ask how your day was without prompting. You waited for him to notice the things you'd stopped mentioning because you didn't want to feel like you were nagging. You waited for him to morph into the partner you deserved, all the while bending yourself into someone who seemed easier to love.

And then, one day, clarity hit—maybe while folding his shirt that somehow ended up in your laundry, or staring at your phone after another unanswered message. You realized you weren't in love with *him*. You were in love with his potential, the man you thought he could become if only he tried a little harder, cared a little more, grew a little faster. The emotional rollercoaster of holding onto that potential left you exhausted, questioning if you were too demanding, too high-maintenance, too much.

But let's set the record straight: asking to be seen, heard, and valued isn't asking for too much. It's asking for the very baseline of what love should be. You're not high-maintenance for expecting respect. You're not too much for needing reciprocity. And here's the truth no one tells you: you can't sculpt someone else's growth. You can't pour your love into their empty spaces and expect it to make them whole. Love doesn't work like that. You can offer support, yes, but growth? That's an inside job. And if you're constantly waiting for someone to catch up, you're not in a partnership—you're in a performance, playing the role of fixer, cheerleader, and emotional caretaker all at once.

The IT Girl's Approach To Compatibility

The IT Girl doesn't settle for potential because she understands the value of her time, her heart, and her energy. She knows that compatibility isn't about forcing mismatched pieces to fit—it's the harmony of finding someone whose puzzle naturally aligns with hers, creating something beautiful and whole without sacrificing her edges. Compatibility is built on mutual respect, shared priorities, and a connection that feels natural—a relationship where both people have the freedom and encouragement to grow without one overshadowing the other. It's not about perfection, but about finding someone who meets her where she is and walks alongside her.

The IT Girl doesn't romanticize red flags or mistake love for a project. She's not interested in fixing someone or waiting for them to evolve. Instead, she looks for actions, not promises. Does he show up? Consistently, not just when it's convenient? Does he listen when she speaks, truly hear her, without turning the conversation back to himself? Does he make her feel valued in ways that don't require her to spell it out repeatedly? If the answer is no, she doesn't waste her time second-guessing herself. She's learned that lingering in the hope of potential is like waiting for a train at a station that's already closed—a futile exercise that leads nowhere.

What sets the IT Girl apart is her unwavering sense of self-worth. She moves through life with the confidence that she doesn't need to beg for love or settle for breadcrumbs. When she walks away from someone who doesn't meet her standards, she doesn't see it as a loss—she sees it as making space for someone who will. She trusts her intuition to guide her, knowing that love isn't meant to feel like a struggle or a compromise of her identity. It's meant to enhance, not deplete.

She's mastered the art of staying in her power. When someone comes into her life, they're not met with desperation or a desire to prove her worth—they're met with a quiet, unshakable strength. She doesn't chase, she attracts. And the ones who recognize her value? They show up fully, without excuses or hesitation. The IT Girl doesn't just hope for love; she embodies the kind of love she wants to receive, and in doing so, she sets the standard for how she is treated.

She's not afraid of walking away because she knows that walking away from what doesn't serve her is an act of walking toward what does. She's learned that settling for potential isn't just a waste of time—it's a disservice to herself. And an IT Girl never compromises on the masterpiece she's creating with her life.

What To Do: A Sacred Practice

Here's the secret to breaking free from the potential trap: focus on the present. Tonight, create a space just for you—dim the lights, light a candle, and sit with your thoughts. Close your eyes and envision your ideal partner. Not their potential, but how they make you feel today. Do they prioritize you? Do they match your energy? Do they add joy and ease to your life? Now, shift the focus to yourself. Picture the version of you who no longer waits for someone to change. What choices does she make? How does she spend her time? Meditate on her confidence and clarity. Let her guide your next steps.

Then, write down your non-negotiables. Be specific. What do you need in a partner right now? Respect? Consistency? Emotional availability? Stick to this list like your happiness depends on it—because it does.

Now, take it further. Reflect on how you've shown up in past relationships. Were you authentic, or were you dimming your light to fit someone else's comfort? Write it all out. Clarity begins with honesty. And with clarity, you'll find that you're not just creating space for the right partner—you're also creating a stronger, truer version of yourself.

The Profound Truth About Love

Love isn't about potential—it's the presence of someone who meets you where you are, not the promise of someone who might catch up someday. The IT Girl doesn't gamble her heart on maybes. She chooses someone who already knows how to value her, because she values herself too much to settle for less.

And if you've been holding onto someone for who they might become, ask yourself this: *Would you choose them exactly as they are today?* If the answer is no, it's time to let go. Because real love doesn't ask you to wait, to fix, or to settle. Real love meets you in the now, where you are fully seen, deeply valued, and never asked to dim your light.

Darling, remember this: potential is the illusion, but compatibility is the truth. Choose the truth every single time.

Balancing Vulnerability With Self-Protection: Sharing Your Heart While Maintaining Boundaries

Vulnerability. It's a word that gets thrown around like it's the secret ingredient to an ideal life—celebrated in theory, but so often misunderstood in practice. People tell you to "open up," to "be yourself," as though baring your soul is as simple as flipping a light switch. But let's get real: vulnerability isn't a carefully crafted Instagram post or a casual overshare during happy hour. It's raw. It's brave. And, when handled carelessly, it can cut deeper than rejection. The IT Girl understands this better than anyone. She knows that vulnerability is a strength, but only when wielded with discernment.

Vulnerability without boundaries is like leaving your front door wide open, hoping only the right people walk in. It's risky, and more often than not, it's a gamble that leaves you exposed. The IT Girl doesn't gamble with her heart. She's learned the delicate art of balancing openness with self-protection, of peeling back her layers one at a time, only for those who've shown they're worthy of seeing what's underneath. Vulnerability, for her, is a slow dance, not a reckless leap—a way to connect without losing her sense of self.

The Dance Of Vulnerability And Boundaries

Now consider this: you've just met someone. The chemistry is undeniable, a spark that makes you feel alive in ways you hadn't realized you'd missed. Every interaction feels like an invitation to dive deeper, to share the pieces of yourself you usually keep locked away. You're tempted to lay your heart bare—to reveal every dream, fear, and heartbreak you've ever carried, all in the name of connection. But here's the pause you need: *Have they earned the privilege of that access?* Vulnerability does not hinge on throwing open the floodgates of your emotions and hoping the other person knows how to swim—it's the careful act of testing the waters first, ensuring they're capable of holding space for what you bring.

The IT Girl doesn't confuse chemistry with trust. She shares herself in stages, like unwrapping a carefully folded letter. Each layer reveals something more profound, but only when she feels it's safe. She'll drop a hint about her passions or share a small piece of her past, then step back and observe. Do they lean in with curiosity? Do they reflect back understanding? Or do they brush it off, dismissing her depth in favor of their own agenda? For her, vulnerability is a dance—a rhythmic back-and-forth that builds intimacy without compromising her emotional well-being.

And let's talk about boundaries. Boundaries are not barriers; they're invitations. They say, *This is how I need to be treated to feel respected. This is the standard I've set for myself.*

Boundaries aren't about shutting people out; they're about creating an environment where mutual respect and connection can flourish. When you set boundaries, you're not building walls to keep people away—you're setting the stage for the right people to step in closer, fully prepared to honor your value and meet you where you are.

Boundaries also give you the power to pause and evaluate without guilt. Instead of rushing into vulnerability, the IT Girl uses her boundaries as a litmus test. Does this person listen, or do they interrupt? Do they ask questions that deepen the conversation, or do they redirect it back to themselves? These moments of observation aren't just about protecting her peace; they're about preserving the parts of herself that are too precious to be mishandled. Vulnerability, when paired with boundaries, becomes not just a strength but a tool for creating authentic, balanced relationships.

The Danger Of Over-Sharing

We've all been there. You're sitting across from someone who feels like magic, their words wrapping around you like a warm blanket, making you believe, just for a moment, that they're the one you've been waiting for. You lean in, sharing your dreams, your fears, your scars, and your secrets as if opening up will bring you closer. At first, it feels liberating, like shedding a heavy coat on a warm day. But as the relationship evolves—or doesn't—a small voice creeps in: *Did I share too much? Did they earn the right to hold these pieces of me?* Suddenly, what once felt freeing now feels exposing. You're left wondering if you've given away parts of yourself that can't easily be reclaimed.

This is the danger of over-sharing, and it's a trap so easy to fall into when the chemistry is undeniable. But remember: vulnerability isn't about throwing open the doors to your soul and hoping for the best—it's an act of discernment. The IT Girl understands this deeply. For her, vulnerability isn't a desperate plea for connection; it's a deliberate act of trust. She doesn't share to fill silences or seek validation. She shares to create intimacy with those who have proven they're worthy of it. And when the connection isn't mutual, she's not afraid to pull back. Not with anger, not with regret, but with the quiet confidence of someone who knows her worth.

Because here's the truth: your story is yours to tell, but it's also yours to protect. Not everyone you meet deserves a front-row seat to your life. The IT Girl doesn't see vulnerability as an open bar; she sees it as a curated experience. But remember: vulnerability isn't about throwing open the doors to your soul and hoping for the best—it's an act of discernment. The IT Girl understands this deeply. They're for those who have shown, through their actions and their consistency, that they can be trusted to hold your truths with care.

How To Balance Openness With Self-Protection

1. **Start Small**: Vulnerability doesn't mean laying everything bare at once. Share a little, then observe. How does the other person respond? Do they ask questions? Do they show empathy? Or do they brush it off and change the subject? Let their actions guide your level of openness.

2. **Define Your Boundaries**: Before you go into any relationship, romantic or otherwise, decide what you're comfortable sharing and what you're not. Maybe you're okay talking about your dreams, but your past heartbreaks are off-limits until trust is established. Stick to these boundaries like your peace depends on it—because it does.

3. **Check In With Yourself**: After spending time with someone, ask yourself how you feel. Energized? Safe? Or drained and uneasy? Your body often knows what your mind hasn't processed yet. Pay attention to those feelings; they're your internal compass.

4. **Communicate Clearly**: Boundaries aren't just about what you won't share; they're about what you expect in return. If someone crosses a line, address it immediately. The IT Girl doesn't let resentment fester in silence. She speaks up, calmly and confidently.

The Secret To Protecting Your Peace

Here's the best-kept secret about balancing vulnerability and boundaries: it's not driven by fear—it's built on trust. Trusting yourself to know when to share and when to hold back. Trusting your instincts to guide you toward people who deserve your openness. And most importantly, trusting that the right connections don't require you to sacrifice your sense of self.

Think of vulnerability as a candle. When shared with care, it lights up the room, creating warmth and intimacy. But without boundaries, it's a flame that can burn out quickly, leaving you feeling exposed and empty. The IT Girl knows how to keep her candle burning—bright enough to invite others in, but protected enough to withstand the winds of life.

And here's the final piece of advice, the one you won't find in any self-help book: never let someone's inability to hold your vulnerability make you feel like you should stop sharing. The problem isn't your openness; it's their lack of capacity. The IT Girl doesn't close off her heart because of one wrong person. She simply saves her light for those who know how to cherish it.

What This Means For You

The IT Girl approach to relationships is never about playing games or keeping walls up—it's the freedom to show up fully as yourself, with the confidence to walk away from anything that doesn't honor your worth. It's loving deeply without losing your identity, setting standards without apology, and seeing rejection not as a setback, but as a stepping stone to something greater.

This isn't just about dating—it's a way of living. It's the intentional creation of a world where your peace, your joy, and your self-respect come first. It's the deep understanding that real love, when it's right, will never require you to compromise the most important relationship of all—the one you have with yourself.

So, ask yourself: Are you loving with intention, or are you losing yourself in the process? Are you holding onto potential, or are you honoring what's real? Are you setting boundaries, or are you letting people dictate your worth?

The answers to these questions will shape not just your relationships, but your entire life. And the IT Girl? She knows the answers. She lives them. She thrives because of them.

Non-Negotiables And Standards

How To Identify Your Non-Negotiables

I want to get back to your non-negotiables. Let's dive into the real work: figuring out what truly matters to you. Not the curated version of what society says you should want, not the polished checklist your friends swear by, and certainly not what an ex tried to convince you was "good enough." This is about you—raw, unfiltered, and unapologetically yourself. It's the process of shedding external expectations and getting brutally honest about what you truly need to thrive in a relationship. Where does this kind of clarity come from? Your past. The heartbreaks you've endured, the sacrifices you've made, the compromises that left you feeling hollow—they're the breadcrumbs leading you to the truth of what you'll never settle for again.

But here's the nuance most people miss: understanding the difference between a non-negotiable and a preference. This isn't just about drawing lines in the sand—it's the distinction between the foundation and the decor, knowing what truly matters versus what's merely surface-level. Non-negotiables are the bedrock—the must-haves that ensure a relationship doesn't just survive but thrives. Preferences, on the other hand, are the cherry on top—the details that make a relationship delightful but aren't essential to its core. The IT Girl knows the difference. She knows that letting go of preferences is compromise, but letting go of non-negotiables is self-abandonment.

This isn't work for the faint of heart. It means revisiting the moments that made you question your worth—the nights you stayed up agonizing over someone who wouldn't text back, the times you bent over backwards trying to save a relationship that was already crumbling, the heartbreak of giving more than you ever received. Those memories hurt, but they're also the key. Because in every tear, in every whispered "never again," lies your power. Each disappointment becomes a lesson, each heartbreak a roadmap. And the IT Girl? She doesn't just skim over these lessons. She studies them like her life depends on it—because it does.

Let's break it down further. Non-negotiables are rooted in your values—the things that define how you live and love. They're the qualities that make you feel safe, respected, and seen. Think emotional availability, integrity, mutual respect. Preferences, though? They're the surface-level details—a love for the same movies, a shared hobby, or a specific lifestyle. Preferences can enhance compatibility, but they can't sustain it. The IT Girl doesn't waste time conflating the two. She knows that while preferences can make someone interesting, non-negotiables make them worth investing in.

Letting go of the pain and guilt attached to these memories is a necessary part of this process. Here's the hidden truth no one tells you: you don't have to carry the weight of your past to move forward. Instead, you use it. You let it sharpen your vision, clarify your needs, and build the kind of unshakable self-respect that sets the standard for what you deserve. And when someone doesn't meet those non-negotiables? The IT Girl doesn't flinch. She walks away, knowing she's not losing; she's making space for what's aligned. She's mastered the art of transforming her wounds into wisdom, her heartbreak into boundaries, and her regrets into clarity. Because she knows the love she deserves isn't just a hope—it's a standard.

Step 1: Reflect On Your Past Relationships

Your past is a goldmine of wisdom—even the parts that make you cringe. Every relationship you've had, whether it ended in heartbreak, frustration, or relief, holds breadcrumbs leading you to your non-negotiables. The red flags you ignored? The compromises that drained you? The moments you felt unseen or unheard? They're not just painful memories—they're signposts. Each one pointing you toward what you need to feel safe, valued, and loved.

Think about it. What moments made you feel cherished, like you were seen for exactly who you are? What made you feel small, like you had to shrink yourself just to keep the peace? Were there patterns that played out in more than one relationship? Maybe it was a lack of communication. Maybe it was always being the one to initiate or put in the emotional work. Or maybe it was something quieter, like never feeling like your opinions carried weight. These aren't random misfortunes—they're lessons etched into your story, waiting to be acknowledged and used.

But the thing about lessons: they demand action. The beauty of understanding these patterns is that you don't have to repeat them. They're not meant to leave you bitter; they're meant to leave you better.

Here's Your Task:

1. Take a moment to reflect on your last significant relationship. Be honest with yourself. What moments brought you joy? What moments broke your spirit?

2. Write it down. Yes, put pen to paper. There's something deeply transformative about seeing your thoughts laid bare. Clarity comes when you can look at your experiences and pull out the threads of what worked and what didn't.

3. Identify the qualities or behaviors that were missing but would've made all the difference. For instance, if you always felt like you were carrying the emotional weight, emotional availability might be one of your non-negotiables moving forward.

The IT Girl doesn't just survive her past; she learns from it. She transforms those lessons into a blueprint—a fortress of self-respect that protects her from settling. She doesn't dismiss her heartbreaks as failures. Instead, she mines them for wisdom, using what she's learned to set the standard for the love she deserves. And here's the kicker: when someone new enters her life, she doesn't throw that blueprint out the window. She holds it close. It becomes her guide, her compass, a way to measure whether this person truly deserves a seat at her table.

This has nothing to do with being cold or rigid. It's about knowing your worth. The IT Girl doesn't confuse potential with compatibility, and she certainly doesn't mistake red flags for fixer-upper opportunities. She knows that each lesson from her past wasn't just a scar—it was a stepping stone toward a relationship where she can finally exhale, knowing she's fully seen and fully loved.

Step 2: Define Your Personal Values

Here's the truth: non-negotiables aren't just about relationships. They're about who you are at your core—what you stand for, what you live by, and what you need to feel whole. They're not arbitrary demands; they're rooted in the deepest parts of you—your values, your experiences, and the lessons you've carried forward.

Ask yourself: What truly fuels you? What gives you a sense of stability and peace? If ambition is what drives your soul, a partner who is complacent will only stifle your growth. If honesty is your cornerstone, even the smallest lie will feel like an earthquake, shaking the very foundation of your trust. Your values are your compass, the true north that guides you, and your non-negotiables? They're the map—a detailed guide to where you're going and what you need along the way.

Here's where it gets complicated—and often misunderstood. Non-negotiables are your foundation. They are the pillars that hold up the architecture of a healthy relationship. Preferences, on the other hand, are the details—the color of the walls, the decor that makes the space feel uniquely yours. Preferences can make someone intriguing, but they'll never make them a good partner. The IT Girl understands this distinction with razor-sharp clarity. She knows that letting go of preferences is flexibility, but letting go of non-negotiables? That's self-abandonment.

You've met someone who seems like the answer to every "what if" you've ever whispered into the universe. They're magnetic—the kind of person who can turn a mundane Tuesday into magic with their charm. They make you laugh, they're impossibly engaging, and they've memorized all the lyrics to the same obscure indie songs you've cherished since college. At first, it feels like serendipity. But then, the cracks begin to show. They brush off your concerns with a joke that stings more than it soothes. They dodge difficult conversations as if acknowledging your needs is too heavy a task. You tell yourself, *But we share so much... They're fun, they're kind, they get me.*

And yet, deep down, there's an ache you can't ignore—a quiet knowing that their charm doesn't fill the void where respect and understanding should live. This is the moment where the IT Girl steps in—where she chooses herself over potential. Because no amount of shared playlists, laughter, or charm can replace the grounding force of alignment. She knows her worth, and she knows the difference between compromise and self-betrayal. That's why she lets go—not out of anger or bitterness, but out of clarity and love for herself.

The Power Of Honoring Yourself

Valuing your standards is an act of radical self-love. It's the moment you stop bargaining with your worth and start recognizing that you deserve to stand tall, unwavering, in what you know you need. This isn't just about relationships—it's the commitment to living boldly, unapologetically, and in full alignment with who you truly are. The decision to stop settling for less isn't easy, but it's transformational. When you honor your standards, you send a signal to the world that says, "This is what I'm worth, and I will accept nothing less." And the world? It rises to meet you.

Setting The Tone IT Girl Style

The way you love sets the tone for your entire life. It's more than just romance—it's the legacy you create. Love, at its core, isn't about searching for someone to complete you or molding someone to fit your world—it's the reflection of how deeply you honor yourself and the connections you allow into your life. Love is about creating a life that mirrors your values, amplifies your peace, and feels like an extension of your highest self. And let me be clear, this isn't the watered-down, Hallmark version of love. This is the real, soul-deep kind of love that transforms—not because of the person you're with but because of the person you become in its presence.

The IT Girl doesn't love on autopilot. She doesn't fall for the façade, the potential, or the performance. She loves with intention, with eyes wide open and standards set high. And here's the truth that's equal parts uncomfortable and empowering: the way you allow yourself to be loved defines the legacy you leave behind. So why settle for crumbs when you deserve a feast? This isn't just about relationships—it's the act of rewriting your story. It's stepping into the kind of love that aligns with your values, honors your boundaries, and elevates your life. It's the transformation into the IT Girl who understands that love isn't something you chase—it's something you embody.

Let's dive in.

How Setting High Standards Builds Long-Lasting Emotional Satisfaction

Love isn't just an emotion. It's a force—a quiet, life-altering energy that seeps into every corner of your existence. The right kind of love doesn't just make you smile; it shifts your perspective, recharges your spirit, and renews your sense of self. It's the difference between surviving and thriving. But you should know that—real, soul-enriching love doesn't just happen. It's cultivated, chosen, and built on the foundation of respect, alignment, and authenticity. A healthy relationship isn't just a luxury; it's a necessity. Love isn't measured by grand gestures or cinematic declarations—it's found in the steady undercurrent of care that keeps you grounded, joyful, and whole. Let's talk about the kind of love that doesn't just fill a void but builds a sanctuary—a love that doesn't deplete but replenishes.

Mental Clarity: Love That Clears The Fog

A truly healthy relationship doesn't just feel good; it makes sense. It's like stepping out of a noisy room into the serene quiet of nature. Suddenly, the mental gymnastics you've been used to performing—deciphering texts, overanalyzing tone, replaying arguments in your head—vanish. Love like this clears the fog. It doesn't leave you questioning your worth or your place in someone else's life.

Think about this: a partner whose words and actions align so seamlessly that you never have to second-guess their intentions. They say they'll call, and they do. They promise to show up, and they're there. This kind of love creates mental peace because it eliminates uncertainty. It's not the absence of challenges—it's the removal of unnecessary chaos.

Contrast that with a relationship where every interaction feels like a puzzle you're desperate to solve. The late-night arguments that loop in your mind, the mixed signals that leave you spinning, the constant questioning of whether you're asking for too much. That's not love—it's emotional turbulence disguised as passion. Real love? It feels like a deep exhale after holding your breath for far too long.

Emotional Security: Love That Grounds You

Healthy love doesn't just touch your heart; it anchors it. It's the kind of connection that feels like planting your feet firmly on solid ground after years of being swept away by waves. Emotional security isn't flashy; it's steady. It's knowing that you can be vulnerable—truly, unapologetically yourself—without fear of judgment or rejection.

Imagine being with someone who doesn't just tolerate your flaws but embraces them. Someone who listens when you're scared, celebrates when you're proud, and holds space when you're unsure. Emotional security doesn't come down to fixing each other—it's the creation of a safe haven where both of you can grow. It's the kind of love that gives you permission to be both a masterpiece and a work in progress.

But time for a reality check: many of us have experienced the opposite. The kind of relationship where your vulnerability is met with indifference or, worse, used against you. Where you're treading carefully, afraid that one misstep could lead to an explosion. That's not emotional security—that's emotional exhaustion. Love that grounds you doesn't uproot your peace; it nurtures it.

Physical Renewal: Love That Heals

Here's a truth we don't talk about enough: love has a profound impact on your body. A toxic relationship doesn't just hurt your heart—it wears down your entire system. Sleepless nights, stress-induced headaches, that constant knot in your stomach—all signs that your relationship might be taking more from you than it gives.

But the right kind of love? It's restorative. It helps you sleep deeper, breathe easier, and feel more energized. Healthy love soothes your nervous system. It replaces tension with comfort, anxiety with calm. Imagine going to bed each night feeling secure in your relationship—no lingering arguments, no racing thoughts, just peace. That's what love should feel like.

Think about the moments when your partner does something small but deeply considerate—like running their fingers through your hair when you're overwhelmed or showing up with your favorite snack after a tough day. Those gestures aren't just sweet; they're healing. They remind your body that it's safe, cherished, and cared for.

The Harmony Of Alignment: When Love Reflects Your Values

Here's the thing that most people miss: the most fulfilling relationships aren't built on passion alone—they're built on alignment. When your partner shares your values, supports your dreams, and respects your boundaries, love stops being a struggle and starts being a flow. It's not about agreeing on every detail—it's the alignment of moving through life with a shared sense of purpose.

Envision this: a relationship where your partner doesn't just tolerate your ambitions but champions them. Someone who doesn't just respect your boundaries but encourages them. That's alignment. Finding love isn't a matter of checking every box on a list—it's the process of building a partnership where both of you feel seen, supported, and celebrated.

Alignment doesn't mean being without conflicts. It means knowing that even when disagreements arise, there's a foundation of respect and shared goals to return to. It's the intentional creation of a relationship where both people feel empowered, not diminished. And when you find that kind of love, it's transformative.

The Joy Of Being Fully Seen

There's nothing more liberating than being loved for who you truly are—not for who you think you need to be. When your relationship aligns with your values, it becomes a space where you can exhale. You're not performing or pretending. You're just existing—fully, authentically, unapologetically. And that kind of connection? It's rare, it's precious, and it's worth waiting for.

Imagine being with someone who lights up when you walk into the room, who listens to your stories as if they're the most fascinating thing they've ever heard, who makes you feel like the most extraordinary person in the world—not because you're trying to be, but because you just are. That's the joy of authentic connection. It's not about finding someone who completes you—it's the discovery of someone who enhances the fullness of who you already are.

The Impact Of Healthy Relationships On Mental, Emotional, And Physical Well-Being

Let's talk about the ripple effect of a healthy relationship. Love isn't just an emotional experience—it's a full-body, full-life phenomenon. When you're in a relationship that aligns with your values, it doesn't just improve your mood—it elevates your entire existence. Here's how:

Mental Peace: Love That Quiets The Noise

A healthy relationship is like a deep exhale after holding your breath for too long. It quiets the endless "what ifs," silences the need to decode mixed signals, and gives your mind the space to rest. When someone's actions align with their words, when they show up consistently and without conditions, your mind stops spinning. And that mental clarity? It's priceless.

Now, picture the opposite. The late-night arguments that replay in your head. The text messages you reread, trying to decipher meaning. The mental gymnastics of wondering, "Am I asking for too much?" That's not love; that's a drain on your peace. Real love doesn't feel like a riddle—it feels like an answer.

Emotional Stability: Love That Grounds You

When you're in a relationship where your emotional needs are met, it's like planting your feet on solid ground after years of walking on shifting sand. You can share your dreams, fears, and flaws without fear of judgment. Emotional security creates a ripple effect of confidence—it makes you stand taller, dream bigger, and love yourself deeper.

Contrast this with a relationship that keeps you off-balance. The kind where you're stepping lightly, trying to avoid setting off a fight. Or worse, the kind where your vulnerability is met with indifference. Healthy love grounds you; unhealthy love uproots you.

Physical Well-Being: Love That Heals

Here's something we don't talk about enough: love impacts your body. A toxic relationship takes a toll—sleepless nights, tension headaches, that pit-in-your-stomach anxiety that just won't quit. But healthy love? It soothes. It helps you sleep better, stress less, and feel more energized. When your relationship feels like a sanctuary, your body thanks you for it.

The Joy And Peace That Come From Living A Love Life Aligned With Your Values

I've talked about this earlier but I really want you to understand that the goal isn't just love—it's alignment. When your relationship reflects your values, life feels less like a struggle and more like a flow. There's an ease to it, a harmony that comes from knowing you're building a life with someone who sees the world the way you do.

Alignment isn't defined by agreeing on every little thing—it's the deep connection of being rooted in the same soil. It's the certainty that your partner shares your vision for love, life, and happiness. When you're aligned, there's no constant push and pull, no battle to make them see your perspective. Instead, there's respect for your individuality and a shared commitment to your collective goals.

There is peace in alignment. It's knowing that you don't have to perform or pretend to be someone you're not. You can show up as your full, unfiltered self and still be loved fiercely. Because there is nothing more liberating than being loved for who you are—not who you're trying to be. When your relationship aligns with your values, it becomes a space where you can exhale. You're not chasing validation or walking on thin ice; you're simply existing, fully and authentically. And that kind of connection? It's rare, it's precious, and it's worth every second of waiting for the right person.

The Intimacy Of Self-Growth In Love

Here's the paradox about love that no one likes to admit: it's less about finding someone else and more about finding yourself. For the IT Girl, love isn't just an external connection; it's the ultimate internal exploration. Relationships become mirrors, and in their reflection, she sees it all: her strengths, her fears, her capacity to love, and the boundaries she's too afraid to set.

Why Love Is Your Greatest Self-Discovery Tool:

1. **It Tests What You're Willing To Accept:** True intimacy asks you to face your discomfort. Vulnerability forces you to confront what you've allowed in the past and what you refuse to allow moving forward. Love challenges you to honor your boundaries—even when it's hard.

2. **It Sharpens Your Self-Awareness:** Every relationship teaches you something new about yourself—your triggers, your needs, and your capacity for compassion. Love asks you to look inward and acknowledge the patterns you've outgrown.

3. **It Pushes You To Grow:** The right relationship doesn't fix you; it inspires you. It encourages you to step into the best version of yourself, not for someone else, but because you've realized what you're capable of.

But here's the secret: this growth isn't for anyone else. It's not about becoming who someone wants you to be; it centers on evolving into the woman you've always been destined to be. And the right person? You don't bend yourself to fit into someone's life. Instead, you stretch into your own potential, knowing that any relationship worth having will amplify your individuality, not erase it.

The Balance Of Independence And Connection

The IT Girl knows one undeniable truth: love isn't wrapped up in giving up parts of yourself to make room for someone else. It's the creation of a partnership where both lives remain vibrant, full, and unapologetically individual. She doesn't dissolve into the relationship—she enhances it, and it enhances her.

How You Balance Love And Independence:

1. **Your Life Remains Your Priority:** Your career, your friendships, your passions—these are the pillars of who you are. A relationship doesn't overshadow

them; it enhances them. You don't rearrange your world for someone else—you invite them into it.

2. **Mutual Effort Is Non-Negotiable:** Love is a partnership, not a one-person show. You give, but you expect to receive. If the scales tip too far in one direction, you're not afraid to walk away.

3. **Solitude Is Your Sanctuary:** Time alone isn't lonely; it's restorative. You treasure the moments where you reconnect with yourself, ensuring that no matter how deep your connection with someone else, you never lose sight of who you are.

Love, for you, is an addition, not a subtraction. It's not about shrinking yourself—it's the expansion of who you are, together.

Building A Love That Honors Her Growth

You, as the IT Girl, know that love isn't meant to hold you in place; it's meant to elevate you. A partnership worth your time and heart is one that grows with you, not against you. It's not about fitting someone else's mold or settling for what's easy—it's the creation of something meaningful, dynamic, and deeply connected.

Your Vision For Love:

1. **Being Crystal Clear About What You Want:** Whether it's a long-term partnership, a shared life of adventure, or the kind of relationship where you grow individually and together, clarity is your foundation. You deserve someone who's not just aligned with your goals but enthusiastic about them.

There's no room for ambiguity or half-hearted effort.

2. **Embracing Healthy Conflict:** Disagreements don't scare you; they're invitations to understand each other better. For you, the IT Girl, conflict isn't about winning or losing—it's the pursuit of solutions that honor both your voices. The right partner sees challenges as a chance to grow closer, not as a reason to pull away.

3. **Making Joy Non-Negotiable:** Love should feel expansive. It's not just about sharing responsibilities or navigating life's complexities—it's the ability to find laughter in the chaos and create moments that feel effortless. Love, at its core, should bring lightness and connection, even in the midst of life's heavier moments.

You deserve love that complements your evolution—a relationship that feels like a steady rhythm, not a dissonant tune. And as you continue to step into your power, that vision will not only guide you but ensure you never settle for anything less than what makes your heart feel alive.

The IT Girl's Love Decree

You, the IT Girl, know that love is not tied to settling—it focuses on stepping into something that feels expansive, fulfilling, and completely aligned with who you are. You've done the work. You've felt the heartbreak, rebuilt the pieces, and emerged stronger, wiser, and more unapologetically yourself. Now, you're ready for love that mirrors the power and beauty of the life you've created.

Repeat To Yourself:

- I will only pursue love that aligns with my values, my peace, and my purpose.

- I deserve a partner who doesn't shrink in the face of my growth but celebrates it with me.

- I refuse to sacrifice my identity or authenticity for the sake of connection.

In all sincerity—stepping back into the world of love after heartbreak is no small feat. It's a dance between vulnerability and strength, hope and caution. But this isn't really about fear—it's grounded in wisdom. It's knowing that you, IT Girl, aren't searching for someone to complete you—you're looking for someone who sees you as whole, who adds depth without requiring you to shrink. The love you seek isn't just a possibility; it's your birthright. And now, with your head held high, it's time to claim it.

The Legacy Of Love That Honors You

When you choose to love like an IT Girl—with intention, with clarity, with high standards—you're not just changing your love life. You're changing your life, period. You're creating a legacy of love that respects, honors, and elevates you. And that legacy? It's not just for you. It inspires every woman who watches you demand more and settle for nothing less.

So here's your call to action: demand better. Love harder. Expect more. Because when you love like an IT Girl, you're not just writing a love story—you're rewriting the rules.

Part 5:
She's Ready

Now Being Ready To Date After Heartbreak

Being ready to date after heartbreak feels like standing at the edge of a brand-new chapter, pen in hand, poised to write a story you're finally ready to star in. It's stepping into sunlight after what felt like an endless storm, soaking in its warmth while still keeping an eye on the clouds. Vulnerability accompanies this phase like a shadow, reminding you of the wounds you've healed and the lessons you've learned. But it's not a vulnerability rooted in fear; it's a quiet strength—a knowing that while the journey left its scars, those scars are proof of survival, not defeat.

Dating after heartbreak doesn't come down to patching yourself up with someone else's attention. It's based on walking into this phase whole, aware of your own worth, and unwilling to compromise the self-love you've painstakingly built. The IT Girl doesn't see dating as a way to fix what was broken but as an opportunity to grow into the woman she's always been capable of becoming. She knows that the storm taught her how to dance in the rain, and now she's ready to waltz in the sun—but only with someone who matches her rhythm.

The IT Girl isn't chasing anyone's approval or validation. She's already stamped her own. She's not searching for a savior; she's seeking a partner—someone who doesn't just walk into her life but fits seamlessly into it, enhancing the masterpiece she's already painted. Heartbreak didn't weaken her; it sharpened her vision. She's discerning now, unapologetically so. Because for her, dating isn't a distraction—it's a deliberate act of self-respect. She's not settling for love that asks her to compromise her standards or peace. She's only making space for the kind that amplifies everything good she's already cultivated.

Nothing To Prove

Dating has nothing to do with proving anything; it's emphasizes showing up as your true self and inviting someone into the life you've built. The IT Girl knows this better than anyone—she doesn't mold herself to fit someone else's expectations or seek approval to feel whole. For her, love isn't a test she has to pass; it's a connection she chooses to explore. It's not about adapting to someone else's preferences or pretending to be less so they feel more comfortable.

The IT Girl knows that a meaningful relationship has no bearing on adjusting her life to someone else's expectations; she welcomes a partner who naturally aligns with the life she's already created. She steps into love with quiet confidence, knowing her worth doesn't hinge on external validation or constant effort to keep someone's attention. Instead, she seeks authenticity—a connection where both individuals can remain true to themselves while building something together. It's not about being without imperfections, but about mutual respect and shared values, where both feel understood and supported without sacrificing their authentic selves.

Rather than compromising her identity for the sake of being chosen, she steps into dating as an equal, ready to learn about someone else but never at the cost of unlearning who she is. This approach isn't about arrogance; it's centered on alignment. It's the belief that the right person will meet her where she stands, without asking her to change who she is.

But stepping into love again after heartbreak is no easy feat. It's a dance between vulnerability and self-preservation. It's your chance to hold the door open to possibility without letting the past sneak in to haunt her. She's healed, she's grown, and now she's stepping out into the world with an armor made of lessons and a heart that's still tender but beating stronger than ever.

This isn't focused on searching for someone to fill a void; she's already enough. It's the connection with someone who understands her depths, admires her strength, and values her individuality. For her, stepping back into the world of dating is less about the pursuit and more about discovery—not of someone else, but of how love fits into the life she's built. This is her time to allow herself to connect while knowing she has the strength to stand tall, even if things don't go as planned. Dating again doesn't mean she's afraid of falling; it means she's confident in her ability to rise every single time.

Stepping Back Into The Arena: Dating With Intentions, Not Expectations

When the IT Girl steps back into the dating world, she's not searching for someone to complete her—she's seeking alignment with someone who complements the life she's already created. It's a shift in perspective: love isn't centered on filling a void or proving her worth; this is her exploring connections that feel right, real, and reciprocal. And the best part? She's doing it on her terms.

Her Refined Approach To Dating:

1. **Each Interaction Is A Learning Curve:** She doesn't rush to define someone as "the one." Instead, she uses dates as opportunities to better understand herself and what she needs in a partner. It's not about putting pressure on every meeting—this is about staying curious and open while remaining grounded.

2. **Substance Over Superficial Sparks:** A spark may light the match, but compatibility is what sustains the fire. The IT Girl is no longer wooed by charm alone; she's looking for depth—shared values, emotional intelligence, and mutual respect. It's not enough to vibe; she's seeking someone who genuinely aligns with her purpose.

3. **Rejection Becomes Her Compass:** When someone isn't a fit, she doesn't dwell on what's missing. Instead, she views it as a redirection toward something better. She's learned that "no" from someone else is often the universe's way of saying, "this isn't for you"—and she's okay with that.

The IT Girl approaches dating with the quiet confidence of someone who knows her worth. She's not auditioning for approval, nor is she shrinking herself to make someone else comfortable. She's showing up, fully herself, because the right person won't need convincing of her value—they'll see it, celebrate it, and meet her there without hesitation.

Why Are You Dating?

Here's a question that deserves more thought than a casual shrug: why are you dating? Not the Instagram caption version, not the response you give your friends when they prod, but the raw, unfiltered truth. Because without clarity, dating becomes an exhausting loop of emotional guesswork—a roulette wheel where you spin, hope, and too often land on disappointment. The IT Girl doesn't gamble with her heart. She's in it for keeps, not consolation prizes.

Dating with intention is a declaration. It's planting your flag and saying, "I know what I want, and I refuse to settle for anything less." It's not about being demanding or difficult; it's the act of being discerning. Time is a non-renewable resource, and emotions aren't a bottomless well. Wandering into the dating world without purpose is like handing someone the keys to your house and hoping they won't wreck the place. The IT Girl has no room for vague connections or half-hearted efforts. She's all in or not in at all.

So why are you dating? Is it because you're bored? Lonely? Trying to prove something to someone who's probably not even paying attention? Or is it because you're genuinely ready to share your life with someone who's worthy of the invitation? The IT Girl knows the answer to this question before she steps into the dating arena, and that's what makes her approach so powerful.

Why Intention Matters

Let's face it: modern dating is messy—like walking through a crowded flea market where everyone is shouting, selling something, but you're not quite sure what you're looking for. It's a whirlwind of swipes, texts, setups, and missed connections, with everyone claiming they're looking for "something real" but few willing to define what that actually means. Apps have turned love into a transaction, setups come with disclaimers, and meeting someone organically feels like a mythical story you tell your friends over wine, followed by laughter and a sigh. Dating today feels like a high-stakes game with no rulebook, and honestly, it's exhausting.

But the truth about chaos: it only thrives in the absence of clarity. Without intention, dating becomes a game of "close enough"—a cycle of swiping right on people who aren't quite right, going on dates that don't light you up, and staying in connections that drain more than they give. And let's be honest: when was the last time "close enough" ever left you feeling fulfilled? Intention is the antidote to all of it. It's the act of sitting down with yourself and deciding, "This is what I want, this is what I deserve, and I refuse to accept anything less."

Here's the profound truth—highlight it, write it on a sticky note, tattoo it on your heart: *Love without intention is like a beautifully wrapped gift with nothing inside.* It may look good on the outside, but it's hollow. Intention transforms dating from a chore into an empowering experience. It's what allows you to say no to the wrong people without regret and yes to the right ones without fear. It's what keeps you from wandering aimlessly through the chaos and instead walking deliberately toward the kind of connection that makes your soul feel seen.

The Problem With Wandering

Wandering through the dating world is like walking through a crowded market without a list. Sure, you might pick up something shiny here and there, but by the time you leave, your bag is full of things you didn't need and empty of the one thing you came for. Dating without intention doesn't mean you're desperate—it means you're drifting. And drifting is dangerous because it convinces you that "good enough" is the best you'll ever get. When you haven't defined what "extraordinary" looks like, it's far too easy to settle for "close enough."

Without intention, it's like you're holding an empty cup, hoping someone else will fill it, only to find they've poured in just enough to keep you thirsty. Mixed signals start to look like clarity, minimal effort feels like love, and inconsistency becomes the thrill you mistake for excitement. You find yourself gripping tightly to someone's potential, convinced that if you just wait a little longer, they'll grow into the person you need them to be. The fact remains: they won't. People don't become who you need; they become who they are. And the longer you wait, the longer you delay finding what you actually deserve.

Here's a quote to tattoo on your heart: "Potential is the prettiest lie we tell ourselves to justify staying in places we were never meant to be." Wandering leaves you depleted because it sets no boundaries, no standards, and no destination. And without those, how can you ever truly know when you've arrived at something real? Intention isn't just a guide; it's your lifeline. It's what keeps you from handing your heart to someone who doesn't know how to hold it and gives you the power to say "no" without fear and "yes" without hesitation.

Soooooo....

She's sitting in a café corner, her favorite latte steaming on the table, and a book she's been meaning to finish resting in her lap. The world outside the window is bustling, but inside, she feels calm for the first time in months. Her phone vibrates. A text from someone she matched with last week. "When can I see you?" She smiles—not because the message sweeps her off her feet, but because she knows she has the power to decide.

She's learned this the hard way: that time is precious, and so is her energy. In the past, she would have rushed to reply, her excitement tangled with anxiety, wondering if this person might be "the one." But not this time. This time, she's in control. She doesn't measure her worth in someone else's attention. Instead, she's discerning. She takes a deep breath, sips her latte, and texts back on her own terms. She's dating with clarity now. She knows her non-negotiables, and she knows how it feels to ignore them—and she's vowed to never do it again.

This is the beauty of dating with intention. It's not about playing games; it's the clarity of knowing the rules of your own heart and staying true to them. She's not searching for someone to complete her. She's inviting someone to share in the life she's already built—on her terms.

There Is A Purpose

Intention is your compass, the North Star that keeps you grounded when the dating world feels like an endless carnival of distractions. Without it, you're spinning your wheels, stuck in a cycle of mixed signals, missed opportunities, and people who don't deserve a second of your precious time. But when you're clear about what you want—and more importantly, what you won't tolerate—something magical happens: you become magnetic. You attract people who see your worth and repel those who don't even deserve a glimpse of it. Isn't that the dream? To stop decoding cryptic texts and start building connections that feel real, unforced, and aligned with who you truly are?

The IT Girl doesn't play guessing games with her heart. She knows that love isn't supposed to feel like solving a crossword puzzle where every clue leaves you more confused than the last. For her, intention is liberation. It's the quiet power of walking away from something mediocre because she knows she's worth the extraordinary. Intention says, "I'm not here to be tested or toyed with; I'm here to be valued."

Here's the truth worth highlighting: *"Intention is the difference between wandering aimlessly and walking with purpose. Without it, you're just a passenger in your own love story. With it, you're the author."* Clarity has nothing to do with being rigid; it pertains to knowing what you deserve and refusing to settle for anything less. And here's the secret: confidence isn't just sexy; it's contagious. The right people will gravitate toward your energy, and the wrong ones will fade into the background—exactly where they belong.

I'm Talking To You About Your Partner Checklist

Now it's time for you to create your partner checklist. Not for Instagram or any other social media platform, not for your friends over brunch, but for you—the woman who has been through enough to know better. This is your moment to sit down, get honest, and decide what you truly need in a partner. Think of this as the blueprint for your heart's future home. No settling, no compromises, no room for anyone who doesn't meet the standards you're about to set.

The truth is you don't get what you want—you get what you accept. That's the unvarnished reality of modern relationships. Every time you compromise on your standards or convince yourself that the bare minimum is "enough," you're essentially handing someone a manual that says, "Here's how to love me less than I deserve." But not anymore. Not today. Starting now, you're designing your partner checklist and finally playing by your rules.

Let's be clear: a checklist isn't about being picky or demanding. It's not some superficial list of height requirements, gym habits, or how they take their coffee. A real partner checklist dives deeper than surface-level preferences. It's a declaration of what you need—not what you want—to feel respected, valued, and fulfilled in a relationship. This also is not about settling for "good enough." It's rooted in setting a gold standard that ensures the love you accept aligns with the love you deserve.

And before anyone rolls their eyes at the idea of a checklist, consider this: you make lists for groceries, for errands, even for what to pack for vacation. So why wouldn't you approach your love life with the same level of intentionality? Love isn't a lottery, and finding the right partner is not based on luck—it's centered on clarity. The IT Girl knows exactly what she's looking for because she's taken the time to define it. Let's create that list, together.

Step One: Creating A Detailed List Of Qualities And Behaviors

Let's start with the foundation: what qualities and behaviors do you absolutely need in a partner? Think of these as the non-negotiables—the bedrock of a relationship that can withstand storms and stand the test of time. Forget what society tells you to prioritize; this is about you. Your life. Your love story.

1. **Emotional Availability:** Emotional availability isn't optional—it's the price of admission for love that thrives. A partner who is emotionally available shows up—consistently. They'll listen without making you feel small, communicate without making you guess, and meet you in vulnerability instead of running from it. Anything less is a dealbreaker.

   Let's call it like it is for a second. Think about the last time someone's emotional unavailability left you spinning. The unanswered texts, the vague responses, the feeling of being left in a haze of uncertainty. Emotional availability is what keeps you from spiraling into the endless abyss of overthinking. You deserve someone who not only meets you where you are but stays there, no questions asked.

2. **Integrity:** Integrity goes far beyond honesty. It's a reflection of alignment between words and actions.

It's showing up when it's inconvenient, telling the truth when it's uncomfortable, and treating people with kindness even when no one's watching. A person with integrity doesn't leave you questioning their motives or loyalty. With them, you feel safe— not just occasionally, but always.

Because this is possible: a partner who says they'll be there at 7 PM and actually shows up at 6:55. No last-minute excuses, no convenient forgetfulness. Integrity isn't just about keeping promises—it's the essence of creating a life where promises don't feel fragile.

3. **Ambition And Drive:** Ambition is not tied to how much money they make or whether they're chasing titles—it's defined by passion and purpose. Do they care deeply about something? Are they motivated to grow? A stagnant partner leads to a stagnant relationship. You deserve someone who inspires you, someone who's moving forward—and invites you to move forward with them.

    Let's say you're planning your life like an empire. A partner without ambition is like someone staring at blueprints but refusing to pick up a hammer. You need someone who's willing to build alongside you, not someone content to sit in the shadows of your spotlight.

4. **Emotional And Intellectual Compatibility:** Are your values aligned? Do their beliefs about love, family, and the future complement yours? Compatibility

does not revolve around agreeing on everything; it's built having a shared vision for the life you're building together. Emotional and intellectual compatibility turn a relationship into a safe haven, not a survival camp.

Think about it: a disagreement doesn't feel like an earthquake with the right person. It feels like a bridge—two sides coming together to find common ground. Emotional and intellectual compatibility means you can debate without it becoming a war zone.

5. **Respect For Boundaries:** A partner who respects your boundaries doesn't push you into uncomfortable situations, guilt-trip you, or demand explanations for your "no." Respect isn't just foundational—it's non-negotiable. Without it, trust crumbles, and without trust, love cannot thrive.

   Remember this: your boundaries are not hurdles for someone to overcome. They're the map to your peace. The right partner doesn't just respect your boundaries—they honor them as if they were sacred.

Step Two: Including Emotional, Intellectual, And Lifestyle Compatibility Factors

Remember the non-negotiables you wrote down pages ago, well it's time to dig deeper. Compatibility isn't just about matching life goals or swooning over the same vacation destinations—it's a journey through the nuances. The quiet, unglamorous moments that seem trivial until they become the reason you're butting heads over breakfast. Let's break it down and explore the intricacies of alignment:

1. **Lifestyle Choices:** Do your daily rhythms sync? Perhaps your ideal morning involves quiet reflection, a warm cup of tea, and time to ease into the day. Now imagine sharing that space with someone who treats the sunrise like a rally cry—music blasting, chaos unfolding. Compatibility isn't just about enjoying similar activities; it's a foundation of respecting each other's natural pace.

   And let's talk health. Are they on the same page when it comes to prioritizing well-being? Whether it's yoga, hitting the gym, or simply valuing a balanced lifestyle, shared habits here aren't just nice—they're necessary. The right partner doesn't just fit into your lifestyle; they enhance it, making every choice feel like teamwork instead of compromise.

2. **Financial Values:** Money may not buy happiness, but financial discord can certainly dim it. Do they share your philosophy on saving and spending? Are they cautious, reckless, or truly aligned with your goals? Imagine planning a future with someone who dismisses the importance of budgeting while you're mapping out savings for your dream home. Financial compatibility isn't all about bank balances—it's centered on shared priorities, mutual respect, and a vision for the future that feels stable.

3. **Conflict Resolution Style:** How do they handle the inevitable disagreements? The ability to resolve conflict with grace is a cornerstone of any strong relationship. Do they communicate, or do they shut down? Do they turn a disagreement into a battle to win, or a bridge to better understanding?

   Now let's picture this: You've had a tough day and a small disagreement spirals into something bigger. The right person doesn't throw up walls or walk away; they lean in and listen. A partner who values resolution over victory creates a safe space where even arguments deepen connection instead of fraying it.

4. **Family Dynamics:** Their relationship with their family can be a window into how they'll approach yours. Are they close, distant, or somewhere in between? Do they respect the importance of your family in your life? It's not just about whether they get along with your parents; it's the shared understanding and valuing the role family plays in the big picture.

   And what about boundaries? Maybe their family is close-knit, but are they able to balance loyalty with independence? These dynamics might not seem critical early on, but they'll matter when it's time to navigate the holidays or decide where to settle down.

5. **Shared Goals:** Let's get serious: Do you want kids? Do they? What about career ambitions, travel plans, or where you'll live? These questions may feel heavy

in the honeymoon phase, but they're essential for long-term harmony. Alignment here is not just about having identical dreams; it's the harmony of building a shared future where both visions thrive.

Imagine falling deeply in love with someone only to realize your dreams of a bustling city life clash with their longing for countryside serenity. It's not about whose dreams win—it's the dance between finding overlap and compromise that feels natural, not forced.

The truth is, compatibility is rarely about the grand gestures. It's in the mornings, the money talks, the arguments, the family gatherings, and the shared dreams that form the fabric of everyday life. The IT Girl knows these details aren't minor—they're the foundation. And when you get them right, everything else has a way of falling seamlessly into place.

A partner checklist is also not predicated on perfection—it's prioritizes alignment. It reflects the act of crafting a vision of the love you deserve and refusing to settle for anything less. The IT Girl doesn't stumble into relationships; she steps into them intentionally, armed with clarity and confidence. Because when you know your worth, you don't just find love—you find the right love.

PARTNER CHECKLIST
The Essentials
(List your essentials here and on the next page.)

- Emotional Availability:
  - Communicates openly and honestly
  - Listens without judgment
  - Comfortable expressing emotions

- Integrity:
  - Their actions align with their words
  - Loyal and trustworthy
  - Takes accountability for mistakes

- Shared Values:
  - Believes in mutual respect and equality
  - Supports your goals and dreams
  - Shares a vision for the future

Write Your Own Essentials:

1.

2.

3.

4.

5.

6.

7.

8.

9.

10.

Intellectual Compatibility

(List the qualities that stimulate your mind here and on the next page.)

- Curiosity:
    - Enjoys learning and growing
    - Respects different perspectives
    - Has personal passions and interests

- Humor:
    - Laughs at your jokes
    - Can be playful and lighthearted
    - Adds joy to mundane moments

What Else Matters Intellectually?

1.

2.

3.

4.

5.

6.

7.

8.

9.

10.

Lifestyle Alignment

(List your must-have day-to-day compatibility here and on the next page.)

- Health & Wellness:
    - Values physical and mental health
    - Respects your fitness or wellness priorities
    - Supports your self-care practices

- Financial Compatibility:
    - Responsible with money
    - Open about financial goals and challenges
    - Aligned on saving vs. spending habits

Add Your Lifestyle Priorities:

1.

2.

3.

4.

5.

6.

7.

8.

9.

10.

PARTNER CHECKLIST

Emotional Vibes

(List how love feels with them here and on the next page.)

- Emotional Safety:
    - Makes you feel seen and heard
    - Validates your feelings
    - Is supportive during hard times

- Respect for Boundaries:
    - Doesn't pressure or guilt you
    - Listens when you communicate limits
    - Honors your independence

What Do You Need To Feel Emotionally Secure?

1.

2.

3.

4.

5.

6.

7.

8.

9.

10.

Fun, Chemistry, And Spark
(Because love should be exciting. List your chemistry must-haves here and on the next page.)

- Adventurous Spirit:
    - Open to trying new things
    - Enjoys shared hobbies or travel
    - Values spontaneity

- Playful and Fun:
    - Can make you laugh
    - Finds joy in simple moments
    - Doesn't take life too seriously

Add Your Chemistry Must-Haves:

1.

2.

3.

4.

5.

6.

7.

8.

9.

10.

Deal-Breakers

(List your absolute "no's.")

1.

___

2.

___

3.

___

4.

___

5.

___

6.

___

7.

___

8.

___

9.

___

10.

___

QUESTIONS FOR SELF-REFLECTION
(Dive deep to clarify your values, desires, and boundaries.)

1. **What qualities do I admire in myself that I also want in a partner?**

_____
_____
_____
_____
_____
_____
_____
_____
_____

2. **How do I want my partner to handle conflicts or challenges?**

_____
_____
_____
_____
_____
_____
_____
_____
_____
_____

3. **What kind of life do I want us to build together?**

_____

_____

_____

_____

_____

_____

_____

_____

_____

_____

4. **What are three lessons I've learned from past relationships?**

_____

_____

_____

_____

_____

_____

_____

_____

_____

_____

5. **What are my biggest fears about love, and how can I overcome them?**

_____

_____

_____

_____

_____

_____

_____

_____

_____

_____

_____

6. **How do I define emotional intimacy, and why is it important to me?**

_____

_____

_____

_____

_____

_____

_____

_____

_____

_____

_____

7. **What are my deal-breakers, and how did I discover them?**

_____

_____

_____

_____

_____

_____

_____

_____

_____

_____

_____

8. **Am I currently showing up as the partner I want to attract?**

_____

_____

_____

_____

_____

_____

_____

_____

_____

_____

_____

QUESTIONS FOR SELF-REFLECTION

(A deeper dive into your relationship goals and self-awareness.)

1. **Do I prioritize my happiness or constantly compromise for others?**

_____

_____

_____

_____

_____

_____

_____

_____

_____

_____

2. **What are three specific ways I want to feel in a relationship?**

_____

_____

_____

_____

_____

_____

_____

_____

_____

_____

_____

3. **Am I ready to receive the kind of love I'm asking for?**

_____

_____

_____

_____

_____

_____

_____

_____

_____

_____

_____

_____

4. **How do I handle rejection or disappointment in dating?**

_____

_____

_____

_____

_____

_____

_____

_____

_____

_____

_____

5. **What role does respect play in my relationships, and how do I define it?**

_____

_____

_____

_____

_____

_____

_____

_____

_____

_____

_____

_____

_____

6. **What hobbies, goals, or dreams have I sacrificed in past relationships?**

_____

_____

_____

_____

_____

_____

_____

_____

_____

_____

_____

_____

7. **How do I envision sharing my life with someone while maintaining my independence?**

_____

_____

_____

_____

_____

_____

_____

_____

_____

_____

_____

_____

8. **What patterns from past relationships do I want to break?**

_____

_____

_____

_____

_____

_____

_____

_____

_____

_____

_____

_____

9. **What does it mean for a partner to be emotionally available?**

_____

_____

_____

_____

_____

_____

_____

_____

_____

_____

_____

10. **What are three qualities I bring to a relationship that I'm proud of?**

_____

_____

_____

_____

_____

_____

_____

_____

_____

_____

_____

Your IT Girl Manifesto

Let's begin with a truth bomb that might make some uncomfortable: you are the masterpiece, not the work-in-progress. Your worth isn't a concept to debate, nor is it a project waiting for someone else's approval to feel complete. Your love story isn't a fleeting subplot in someone else's narrative; it's the headline, the feature presentation. So why do so many of us live like understudies in our own lives, quietly waiting for someone else to hand us the spotlight? Here's the wake-up call: you've always been the main event. You are the IT Girl of your life, and the time to claim that crown isn't tomorrow—it's right now.

Think about everything you've endured—the heartbreaks, the setbacks, the moments you thought would break you but somehow didn't. This has nothing to do with surviving; it's the embodiment of thriving. This chapter is your declaration of independence from self-doubt and external validation. It's the transformation into taking all those lessons life has thrown at you and distilling them into a manifesto for how you will show up in the world moving forward. This isn't just about recognizing what you deserve; it's the bold embrace of owning it. Affirming, without hesitation, that you're worthy of a life that reflects the IT Girl you were always meant to be. You're not here to settle; you're here to set the standard. And darling, the time to do it is now.

Writing a personal manifesto isn't just a task—it's a soul-stirring declaration, a contract with yourself that says: "Never again will I settle for anything less than extraordinary." Think of it as your north star, an unshakable compass guiding you through the moments when life tries to dim your light or make you question your worth. This isn't just a list; it's a love letter to your future self—the woman you're stepping into with every boundary you set, every standard you hold, and every dream you unapologetically pursue.

Start here: Grab your favorite pen—the one that feels like it holds all your secrets—and let's begin your IT Girl Manifesto. On the next page, you will find prompts and spaces to write your truth. Let this be your personal contract, the document you turn to when the world feels shaky, and your worth feels tested.

Your Manifesto Blueprint

1. **Who Are You?** This is where you define yourself, unapologetically. These aren't words for anyone else—just for you. So make them count.

   I am bold, brilliant, and unapologetic about my standards.

   I am deserving of respect, love, and opportunities that match my energy.

   I am magnetic; my presence is a privilege.

   Now, write your truths

   - ○
   - ○
   - ○
   - ○
   - ○
   - ○
   - ○
   - ○
   - ○

2. **What Do You Stand For?** This is your moral backbone, the pillars that hold you steady even when the world tries to shake you.

I stand for honesty, integrity, and mutual respect in all my relationships.

I will never shrink myself to make others comfortable.

I am the architect of my life, and I'll build it with intention.

Now, write what you stand for

- ○
- ○
- ○

3. **What Will You No Longer Tolerate?** This is where you draw the line in the sand. This is about reclaiming your peace, your energy, and your time.

   I will not chase anyone who doesn't value me.

   I will not settle for chaos disguised as love.

   I will no longer make excuses for anyone who doesn't show up for me.

   Now, write what you will no longer tolerate:

   - ○
   - ○
   - ○

4. **Your Daily Promise:** This is your anchor—a ritual that reaffirms your worth every single day. Make it sacred.

Every day, I will choose myself first.

Every day, I will walk into the world knowing I am enough.

Every day, I will honor the woman I am becoming.

Now, write your daily promise

- o
- o
- o

Let your manifesto be your rallying cry. Keep it close—in your journal, taped to your mirror, or whispered to yourself in the quiet moments. It's not just a guide; it's your declaration of worth, your reminder that you are both the masterpiece and the artist, designing a life that feels as incredible as you are.

Embodying The IT Girl Mentality Through Affirmations

Words hold power, especially the ones we speak to ourselves. Affirmations are not just words—they're declarations, sacred promises to yourself about the woman you're becoming. These aren't cliché motivational phrases; they're a mirror reflecting the brilliance, strength, and value you already hold. Speaking them aloud is an act of casting your own spell, a daily reminder that you're not just the IT Girl—you're the prize.

Daily Affirmations For The IT Girl

- "I am the ultimate luxury in my own life; every day, I treat myself as the treasure I am."

- "I attract extraordinary experiences, love, and abundance because they align with my brilliance."

- "I set the tone for how I am cherished by cherishing myself with no apologies."

- "I am elegance personified; my presence turns ordinary moments into celebrations."

- "I honor my happiness by indulging in beauty, joy, and everything that elevates my spirit."

What To Do:

Write these affirmations down in a place you'll see daily—your mirror, your planner, even your favorite handbag. Speak them with intention, as though you're imprinting them onto your soul. But let's take it further. Below are blank spaces for you to create affirmations that reflect your unique journey. These aren't borrowed words; they're yours. Write them, own them, and live them.

Write Your Affirmations:

1.

2.

3.

4.

5.

Pro Tip: Say them out loud each morning—with confidence, with love, with unshakable belief. Let the world adjust to the powerful energy you're putting out. These affirmations aren't just words; they're your sacred script, reminding you that every day is an opportunity to spoil yourself, celebrate yourself, and embrace the IT Girl you were born to be.

Visualizing Your Love Story: Creating The Relationship You Deserve

Here's the truth: love isn't just about finding the right person. It's the embodiment of becoming the person who radiates the kind of love you want. It's not about playing by someone else's rules; it's the intentional design of your own. And that starts with getting crystal clear on what your love story looks like—not the one Hollywood wrapped in a pretty bow, but the one that feels authentic, fulfilling, and uniquely yours.

What Does Your Love Look Like?

Take a deep breath and ask yourself:

- How does your ideal partner make you feel when you're together and when you're apart? Safe? Empowered? Cherished?

- What does your communication feel like—is it easy, open, and mutual? Are they the person who listens with their heart, not just their ears?

- How do they celebrate your wins, support your dreams, and stand beside you during the storms?

- What is the energy of your life together—is it peaceful, exciting, or full of growth?

Now take this further: write it all down. Be specific. The words "loving" or "supportive" are good, but paint the details. Does your ideal partner call just to check in on your big meeting? Do they remember your favorite coffee order? Do they hold space for your bad days without rushing to fix them? Build this picture like it's the most important masterpiece you'll ever create—because it is.

Write Your Love Looks Like Story Here

THE BREAKUP IS A BLESSING

Guided Visualization Exercise

Take five minutes each day—sit quietly, no distractions. Close your eyes and step into your dream relationship, as if it's already your reality. What does it look like?

- Feel your partner's hand in yours as you're walking through the city, both of you laughing like no one else exists.

- See the small gestures: the way they gently brush the hair from your face, the note they left on the counter before work, the way they light up when they see you walk into a room.

- Picture the quiet moments—sipping coffee on a Sunday morning, curled up in a comfortable silence that feels like home.

Let yourself feel the emotions: the calm, the joy, the excitement. These feelings are the roadmap to what you truly desire. The energy you put out in this visualization— the clarity and the belief—is the energy you'll attract back.

Your Visualization Notes:

-
-
-
-
-

Aligning Actions With Your Vision

Here's the catch: visualizing your love story isn't enough. Dreams are wonderful, but they're only as powerful as the steps you take to make them a reality. Alignment is the secret sauce. If you want a partner who's emotionally available, start by nurturing your own emotional availability. If you value ambition in a partner, let that same energy light a fire under your own goals. Remember, you attract what you embody.

It's not about perfection; it's about intention. Love, at its best, reflects the work you've done on yourself. So here's the question: are you showing up as the kind of person you'd want to meet?

What To Do:

- **Audit Your Actions:** Take a good, honest look at your daily choices. Are they aligning with the kind of love you desire? If you want consistency, are you being consistent with yourself? If you crave kindness, are you offering it in abundance—to yourself and others?

  Write It down:
  - o Where am I aligned?

  _____

  _____

  _____

  - o Where am I falling short?

  _____

  _____

  _____

- **Say No To Misalignment:** Let's talk facts: every time you say yes to something that doesn't serve you, you're saying no to what does. If someone's actions don't match their words, or if they're asking you to dim your light to make them shine, walk away. Creating space for the right kind of love starts with letting go of the wrong kind.

What I Need To Release:

- ○
- ○

- **Honor Your Growth:** Choosing yourself and standing by your standards isn't just an act of self-love; it's a revolution in how you show up for your life. Each decision to uphold your worth is a step forward, a mark of the woman you're becoming. Reflect on these moments not just as wins but as milestones of growth.

What I've Grown Through Today:

- ○
- ○
- ○
- ○
- ○
- ○
- ○

When you act in alignment with the love you want, you're not just waiting for the right partner—you're preparing for them. And that preparation? It's the most empowering love story you'll ever write.

You're The Main Character

Your IT Girl Manifesto isn't just a set of rules—it's a declaration of independence. It's the reminder that you are whole, radiant, and powerful beyond measure. It's the compass you turn to when life's chaos tries to pull you off course, the whisper in your ear that says, "You've got this." Because here's the truth: you weren't born to blend in. You're here to take up space, to set the standard, to create a life so rich and fulfilling that love becomes the icing on the cake, not the entire recipe.

This does not hinge on being without flaws; it's rooted in authenticity. It's the bold act of showing up for yourself, every day, and daring the world to keep up. So, my dear, write your manifesto. Live it with every step you take, every boundary you hold, every choice you make to honor your worth. Watch how the world rises to meet you, how doors you never imagined open, how your energy becomes magnetic to everything you deserve.

Because stepping into your IT Girl energy isn't a phase—it's a revolution. And once you've embraced it, there's no turning back. This is your time—claim it, own it, and never look back.

Love That Feels Like Home

Let's clear the air and let's be real about something we've all wrestled with at one point or another: love should never,

ever feel like you're auditioning for a role in someone else's story. It's not about standing under a spotlight, performing to meet impossible standards for applause—or worse, mere acknowledgment. Love—real, gut-wrenching, soul-quenching love—should feel like slipping into your favorite cashmere sweater. Effortless. Warm. It should fit so well, you forget it's even there because it's just...right.

But here's the kicker: so many of us have bought into a version of love that's as comfortable as stiletto heels on cobblestone streets. We've been sold the idea that love means *work*—not the collaborative kind of work where two people build a castle together, but the exhausting grind of trying to convince someone they should *choose* you. The late-night tears, the waiting by the phone, the endless giving without receiving—it's as if we've convinced ourselves that suffering is proof of how deeply we feel. But why, darling, why do we think love needs to hurt to be real?

Let's sit with that for a moment. No one writes love songs about the nights they spent playing it safe. No one pens poetry about the days they felt unseen, unheard, and unappreciated. Because love—the good kind, the right kind—doesn't leave you questioning your worth or holding your breath, waiting for the next emotional landmine to detonate.

Here's where it gets juicy, though. What if the problem isn't them, but the script we've been handed? What if we've been playing a role we were never meant to audition for? Maybe, just maybe, love that feels like home is less about finding someone to complete you and more about building a life that's so damn fulfilling, anyone who enters has no choice but to complement it.

So, let's stop romanticizing the chase, the struggle, the "love conquers all" narrative that makes us believe devotion is measured by how much pain we can endure. Let's talk about what love really *should* look like. It's mutual. It's a little messy but never cruel. It's the kind of love where effort is a two-way street, where conversations are more than just damage control, and where you don't have to shrink yourself to fit inside someone else's limited vision.

And let's not shy away from the tough stuff, because here's the real tea: sometimes, the love we're holding onto isn't the love we deserve. Sometimes, we're so afraid of letting go of the familiar—even when it's bad for us—that we cling to it like a life raft, forgetting that we can swim. But what if letting go isn't the end? What if it's the beginning of something so much better?

This is your mirror moment, my darling. This is where you pause, breathe, and ask yourself: *Is this love truly serving me? Does it honor who I am and who I want to be?* And if the answer isn't a resounding "yes," then maybe it's time to rewrite the script. Because love that feels like home—that real, soul-nourishing, can't-believe-this-is-my-life love—isn't some fairy tale. It exists. But you have to believe you're worthy of it before you can ever find it.

And you should know: you are. You are worthy of the love that doesn't just celebrate you on your best days but holds space for you on your worst. You are worthy of love that doesn't make you prove yourself, chase after it, or bargain for crumbs. You are worthy of love that feels like home—not a fixer-upper, but a palace where you are queen. And queens, my dear, do not settle.

Key Behaviors And Signs That Show Your Ideal Date/Partner Respects And Values You

Let's cut to the chase—without respect, love isn't love. It's theater. A performance where the costumes sparkle, but backstage, the set is crumbling. Respect isn't just the foundation of a relationship; it's the oxygen. Without it, love suffocates, no matter how beautiful it looks from the outside. And I want you to know: respect isn't just about politeness or gestures that look good in public. It's the embodiment of integrity, consistency, and showing up when it matters most.

Respect is about creating space—not just physical, but emotional. It's the kind of space where you're free to be your full self, where your voice carries weight, and your presence is more than tolerated—it's treasured. True respect doesn't flinch in the face of hard truths or falter when things get messy. It's steady, unshakable, and rooted in the belief that love isn't a prize you earn—it's a partnership you nurture.

But let's go deeper. Beyond respect, there's something else that often gets overlooked in the glossy narratives of romance: *reciprocity*. Love without reciprocity is like pouring water into a cup with no bottom—it doesn't matter how much you give; it's never enough. Reciprocity is the quiet undercurrent that keeps love flowing. It's the balance, the give-and-take, the unspoken agreement that both people are equally invested, equally committed, and equally showing up.

The Element Of Reciprocity: Balance Over Bravado

If respect is the frame of a relationship, reciprocity is the rhythm. It's not about keeping score; it's the art of keeping balance. It's the understanding that effort is a two-way street. When you're always the one calling, planning, comforting, and compromising, love starts to feel less like a partnership and more like a job. And to be completely clear: love shouldn't feel like a task on your to-do list. It should feel like collaboration—a dance where both people take turns leading, supporting, and uplifting.

Here's the test of reciprocity: Does your date/partner make you feel like you're rowing the boat together, or are you paddling alone while they enjoy the ride? Do they meet you halfway, or do they only show up when it's convenient? Reciprocity is not tied to grand gestures; it's the quiet strength of small, meaningful actions that say, "I'm in this with you."

The Subtle Art Of Presence

Reciprocity shows up in presence—not just being physically there, but being emotionally engaged. It's the way they look at you when you're sharing something that matters. It's how they ask, "How was your day?" and genuinely care about the answer. It's how they don't just listen—they remember. If someone's presence in your life feels like a cameo instead of a starring role, it's time to ask yourself if they're truly invested.

Here's what to look for:

1. They Show Up Consistently

Consistency is respect dressed in its everyday clothes.

It's not just about remembering your favorite coffee order or following through on a promised date— it's the seamless harmony of actions and words aligned. Imagine coming home after a long day, and your partner has already set up a quiet dinner because they remembered how stressed you were this morning. Or it's the "I'm thinking of you" text sent in the middle of a busy day without needing to be prompted. These small, steady gestures aren't trivial—they're the heartbeat of a relationship that makes you feel seen, heard, and prioritized. It's the foundation of creating a space where you can breathe deeply because you know their actions aren't sporadic; they're intentional. Consistency is not tied to avoiding storms; it's the unwavering presence that provides shelter from them. Imagine this: your partner remembers how you take your coffee, always calls when they say they will, and follows through on even the smallest promises. These aren't just trivial details—they're the bricks that build the trust foundation. It's the "How's your day going?" text on a busy afternoon or showing up when they know you've had a rough week, even if it means rearranging their schedule. Consistency says, "I'm here," in the most tangible, unspoken way possible. It's the reassuring rhythm of someone who makes you feel like a priority every single day—not just when it's convenient. It's the "How's your day going?" text in the middle of a chaotic afternoon, the follow-through on a plan they made with you a week ago, and the reliability that feels like a deep exhale after holding your breath for too long. Consistency doesn't just anchor your heart—it builds the foundation of trust.

When someone values you, they don't leave you dangling in uncertainty, constantly questioning your place in their life. They don't play the guessing game of half-truths or make you feel like an afterthought waiting to be penciled into their schedule. Their consistency is their way of saying, "I see you, I prioritize you, and I'm not going anywhere."

But here's the hard pill to swallow: if their behavior is as unpredictable as New York City weather—gloriously sunny one day and torrential rain the next—what does that really tell you? Chaos isn't love; it's distraction dressed up as intensity. And distraction isn't what you're signing up for. You deserve better than being someone's part-time priority, someone they only show up for when it's convenient. Real love? It's the steady, unwavering kind that lets you rest easy knowing you're valued every single day.

2. They Listen Without Defensiveness

Let's talk about listening—the kind that makes you feel like the most important person in the room.

Let's think about this: you've just had one of those soul-crushing days, the kind where everything feels like an uphill battle, and you sit across from your date/partner at dinner, ready to unload. They lean forward, put their phone face down, and look you directly in the eye. They're not just hearing the words you're saying—they're absorbing them, reading between the lines, and letting you feel the weight of their attention. That's real listening.

Scenario 1: You're unloading about a frustrating workday over dinner. Your date/partner puts their fork down, looks you in the eye, and says, "Tell me more." No interruptions, no defensiveness—just an open invitation to be heard. Then, later, they surprise you with something thoughtful to help lighten your load. That's what it looks like when a date/partner listens to understand, not just to respond. They don't just absorb your words; they act on them. It's not about fixing every problem but showing they care enough to make the effort. Listening without follow-through? That's just noise. Respect means tuning in and stepping up. They lean in, even when the conversation gets uncomfortable. They don't dismiss your feelings with phrases like "It's not that deep." or "Why are you bringing this up again?" Instead, they make space for your concerns, no matter how small or inconvenient.

Now, Scenario 2: you've had a frustrating day at work, and you bring it up over dinner. Instead of brushing it off with a distracted nod or pivoting the conversation back to themselves, they put down their fork, look you in the eye, and say, "Tell me more about what happened. How can I support you?" They don't interrupt; they don't try to fix it immediately; they just hold space for you. And later? Maybe they suggest a way to lighten your load or surprise you with something thoughtful that addresses the issue. That's listening with intention.

And here's the real test: what happens after the conversation? Listening without action is just a performance. Respect means they take what you've said and do something about it. If you've expressed a need—like asking for more quality time or explaining why certain comments hurt—and they genuinely strive to adjust their behavior, that's respect in motion. But if nothing changes, that's not listening—it's lip service. Love that values you doesn't just nod along; it moves mountains to make you feel seen and heard.

3. They Celebrate Your Wins

Real love doesn't just tolerate your success—it *thrives* on it. A partner who values you will be the loudest cheerleader in your corner. They'll celebrate your wins, whether it's a promotion at work, hitting a fitness goal, or finally mastering that impeccable smoky eye. And it won't feel forced or obligatory. Their joy for your success will be genuine because they see your achievements as a reflection of the amazing person they chose to be with.

But what happens when they don't? If their reaction to your victories is lukewarm or, worse, tinged with jealousy, it's time to ask some hard questions. A partner who secretly hopes you'll stumble isn't in your corner—they're competing with you. And competition has no place in love. You deserve someone who sees your glow and thinks, "How lucky am I to be with her?"

4. They Respect Your Boundaries

Boundaries are the sacred guardians of love, the elegant architecture that holds a relationship steady while allowing both partners the freedom to thrive. Boundaries protect your emotional ecosystem—your peace, your energy, your very sense of who you are at your core. They're an act of self-love, a declaration that your well-being is non-negotiable. A partner who values you understands this instinctively. They don't guilt you for needing a night to yourself or for saying no to something that doesn't align with your values. In fact, they admire you for it.

But make no mistake: someone who constantly tests your boundaries or makes you feel like you're asking too much isn't respecting you—they're trying to control you. Respect feels like freedom, not compromise. It's knowing that your "no" is just as valued as your "yes," and that your individuality doesn't threaten the relationship—it strengthens it.

5. They Invest In The Relationship

Love isn't a one-person show where one partner handles all the heavy lifting while the other enjoys the spotlight. It's a duet, a dynamic collaboration where both parties contribute equally to the rhythm and harmony of the relationship. It's the seamless dance of both partners showing up with their unique strengths, sharing the responsibilities, and meeting each other halfway. Picture it like a beautifully choreographed dance—each step, each gesture, is intentional, thoughtful, and balanced. Without this, love loses its spark and tilts into exhaustion, where one person is left juggling too much while the other barely notices the imbalance. A partnership thrives when both partners are invested, engaged, and willing to step into the less glamorous parts of love together, creating a union that feels both supportive and alive. A partner who values you invests in the relationship—emotionally, mentally, and physically. They're willing to have the tough conversations, to make sacrifices, and to put in the work that keeps the relationship growing.

Investment isn't just about romantic date nights or thoughtful surprises (though those are nice); it's the quiet strength of being present in the unpolished moments. It's the partner who sits with you in silence when you're overwhelmed, who offers to help with the tedious or mundane tasks because they know it'll lighten your load. It's the unwavering devotion to supporting you when life feels anything but glamorous, sharing not just in your victories but in your struggles, too. That's the kind of love that builds a foundation of trust and mutual respect. It's the deep commitment to being present when you're stressed, being patient when you're vulnerable, and being persistent when challenges arise. If you're constantly the one holding the relationship together, ask yourself: is this a partnership or a one-woman show?

Why Do These Behaviors Matter?

When someone truly respects and values you, it's not a question—it's a certainty. You feel it in their actions, in the way they prioritize your emotional well-being, and in the quiet moments where their care speaks louder than words. True respect eliminates the guessing games, the endless cycle of overanalyzing texts, and the restless waiting for them to prioritize you. These behaviors—consistency, active listening, celebrating your wins, respecting your boundaries, and investing in the relationship—are the hallmarks of love that fortifies you, not one that leaves you feeling hollow.

But let's flip the lens for a moment: you can't expect to receive respect if you're not giving it to yourself first. The way you let others treat you is a mirror of the standards you set for yourself. If you keep rationalizing poor treatment, swallowing your voice to keep the peace, or accepting crumbs out of fear of being alone, you're signaling to the world that this is all you believe you deserve. And that? That's a story worth rewriting.

Here's the truth: self-respect is the foundation for demanding respect from others. It's the unwavering commitment to holding firm to your boundaries, speaking up for your needs without apology, and walking away from anything that diminishes your worth. Respect isn't a prize you win after proving your value; it's the baseline for anyone who gets to hold a place in your life. And if someone isn't meeting it, you owe it to yourself to stop handing them opportunities to let you down.

Respect isn't something you earn by sacrificing your needs or proving your worth. It's the baseline. And if someone isn't meeting it, they're not your person. Period.

The IT Girl's Standard: What To Demand In Love

The IT Girl doesn't settle for a relationship that's "good enough." She demands love that mirrors the effort, respect, and energy she brings to the table. Here's what that looks like:

1. **Effort:** They're not just present when it's easy—they show up in the hard moments, too.

2. **Respect for Boundaries:** They don't just accept your boundaries; they honor them as an extension of your self-worth.

3. **Celebration, Not Competition:** Your wins are their wins, and their support never feels conditional.

4. **Emotional Safety:** You can be vulnerable without fear of judgment or dismissal.

5. **Consistent Reciprocity:** They match your energy— not just occasionally, but consistently.

The Wake-Up Call: When You're Ready To Fall In Love - Is This Love Worth It?

At the end of the day, love that feels like home is not shaped by perfection— it's defined by presence. It's the quiet power of someone who sees you, chooses you, and stands beside you, not because they need to, but because they want to. And if you're not feeling that? If you're questioning whether you're valued, respected, or celebrated? Then it's time to have the hard conversation—with them and with yourself.

Because love that drains you isn't love. It's compromise at the expense of your joy. And the IT Girl doesn't compromise her peace for anyone. So, here's your reminder: the love you deserve is out there. But first, you have to believe you're worthy of it. Demand more, expect better, and don't stop until you find the kind of love that doesn't just fit into your life but *elevates* it.

The Trusting Of Your Intuition

Let's set the record straight: your intuition is not a whisper to be ignored; it's a roar from the depths of your soul that demands to be heard. It doesn't sugarcoat, and it doesn't wait patiently in the background. It's not paranoia. It's not overthinking. It's your body's way of saying, "Hey, something here doesn't feel right." Yet, how often do we dismiss it for the sake of harmony, peace, or worse, because we're afraid of being labeled as "too much" or "needy"?

Think about it: how many times have you quieted that voice because someone else's explanation sounded more convenient than your gut feeling? You've been there, haven't you? Where you've rationalized their inconsistencies, excused their half-hearted apologies, or ignored the nagging feeling that something was off because it's easier to believe their words than to trust the quiet certainty within you.

Here's the unvarnished truth: your intuition is the most loyal, unshakable friend you'll ever have. It's the friend who pulls you aside at the party and says, "That one? They're no good for you." It sees what your heart isn't ready to acknowledge and what your mind tries to rationalize away. Trusting your intuition is not really about walking around with suspicion in your back pocket; it's the mastery of being so in tune with yourself that you can't be swayed by half-truths or empty gestures. It's the quiet confidence of knowing when something doesn't align with your peace, your values, or your joy—and honoring that without hesitation.

So, let's get into it. How do you tune into that inner voice, especially when love, with all its sparkle and allure, has a way of clouding your judgment? And here's the bigger question: how do you trust the discomfort—the one that warns you, nudges you, or flat-out screams that something isn't right—and not dismiss it as overthinking? Let's break it down into truths that you need to hold close, as close as your favorite red lipstick or your go-to heels. These truths aren't just advice; they're lifelines.

How To Tune Into Your Inner Voice

Your intuition isn't some mystical force reserved for the spiritually enlightened; it's an intrinsic part of you, as natural as your heartbeat. The problem is, we've been conditioned to ignore it. We've been told to "give them the benefit of the doubt," to "not rock the boat," to "not be so sensitive." But tuning into your inner voice does not mean being reactive; it's the quiet mastery of being present enough to notice what your emotions and body are telling you.

1. Start With The Body

Your body is the first responder to emotional danger. A knot in your stomach, a racing heart, a sense of unease you can't quite place—these are your body's alarm bells. If you're sitting across from someone on a date, and everything about the conversation seems fine, but you can't shake the tension building in your chest, pay attention. Your body is picking up on subtleties your mind hasn't processed yet.

For example: You're dating someone who seems impressive on paper. They're charming, attentive, and say all the right things. But every time they talk about their past relationships, there's an edge—a bitterness or a lack of accountability. You feel your stomach tighten, but you dismiss it, telling yourself, "Everyone has baggage." That tightening isn't overthinking; it's your intuition waving a red flag.

2. Notice Patterns, Not Just Moments

Intuition isn't solely about reacting to a single moment; it's the quiet brilliance of connecting the dots over time. Maybe they cancel plans at the last minute, but their excuse sounds valid. Maybe they interrupt you occasionally, but it seems unintentional. Individually, these things might not seem significant, but if your gut keeps tugging at you, it's the invitation to examine the bigger picture. Ask yourself:

- Am I consistently feeling uneasy around this person?
- Do their words match their actions over time?
- Do I feel more or less like myself when I'm with them?

Your intuition thrives in patterns, so don't ignore them.

3. Quiet The Noise

In a world where everyone has an opinion, your intuition can get drowned out by the voices of friends, family, and even well-meaning dating advice. "He's a great guy! Don't overthink it," they'll say. But your intuition doesn't care about their opinion. It cares about your peace.

Take a moment of silence—literally. Turn off the podcasts, mute the group chat, and sit with yourself. **Ask:** How do I feel about this relationship? Not how should I feel, not how do others feel—but what's my truth?

Listening To Discomfort: It's Not Overthinking

Discomfort is the voice of intuition speaking directly to you, but society has a way of training us to silence it. You've heard it before: "Don't be so sensitive," "You're just being dramatic," or the classic, "It's all in your head." But here's the secret: if you're feeling discomfort, it's in your head for a reason.

The "What If" Spiral

Overthinking is when you create problems that don't exist. Intuition is when you notice problems that do. The trick is to differentiate between fear and awareness.

For instance, if you're nervous before a first date, that's fear—it's normal. But if you're in a relationship, and you find yourself feeling like one wrong move and there is no turning back, second-guessing every interaction, or feeling drained after spending time with them, that's discomfort. That's intuition.

The "Is It Me?" Question

We've all been there—wondering if we're the problem. But here's a rule of thumb: if you've communicated your needs clearly, and the discomfort persists, it's not you. It's the situation.

Example: You've told your date/partner that you need more consistency—more communication, more follow-through. They nod, they promise, but their actions stay the same. Your discomfort isn't because you're expecting too much; it's because they're giving too little.

Trusting Your Intuition: A Love Story With Yourself

Trusting your intuition is the ultimate act of self-respect. It's saying, "I believe in my ability to recognize what feels right and what doesn't." And here's the beauty of it: the more you listen to your inner voice, the louder and clearer it becomes.

Actionable Solutions:

1. **Create A Gut Check System:** When something feels off, stop and evaluate. Ask yourself:

   o What is my body telling me right now?

   o Is this feeling consistent, or am I reacting to a one-off situation?

   o Does this align with my values and standards?

2. **Set An Accountability Practice:** Share your intuitive feelings with a trusted friend or mentor—someone who won't dismiss your concerns but will help you unpack them objectively.

3. **Make A Decision Map:** When faced with uncertainty, write down the possible actions and outcomes. Which option aligns with your peace? Which feels heavy? Let your intuition guide you toward clarity.

4. **Honor Small Red Flags:** Don't dismiss little signs of unease. If something feels off, address it early. Have the hard conversation, ask the uncomfortable question, or take a step back to observe.

5. **Practice Self-Validation:** Remind yourself daily: "I trust my ability to discern what is right for me." Build that trust muscle by acting on your intuition in small, everyday decisions.

The Bottom Line

Your intuition is your greatest ally in love. It's not here to scare you; it's here to guide you. It's the compass that keeps you aligned with your values, your peace, and your joy. And when you trust it? You'll find yourself in relationships that don't just look good on the surface but feel good to your soul.

So, tune in. Listen closely. And never, ever dismiss the voice inside you that says, "This doesn't feel right." That voice isn't overthinking—it's wisdom. And wisdom? That's what makes an IT Girl unstoppable in love.

The Declaration Love Is Her Playground, Not Her Proving Ground

Dating isn't centered on proving anything; it's the art of showing up as your true self and inviting someone into the life you've built. The IT Girl knows this better than anyone— she doesn't mold herself to fit someone else's expectations or seek approval to feel whole. For her, love isn't a test she has to pass; it's a connection she chooses to explore. It's not about adapting to someone else's preferences or pretending to be less so they feel more comfortable.

The IT Girl's Guide To Lasting Love: Secrets You Didn't Know You Needed

Let's start fresh, because being the IT Girl does not hinge on how others see you— it's rooted in how you see yourself. It's not about your wardrobe or your beautifully executed plans; it's the quiet confidence of recognizing that love isn't something you have to earn or prove—it's the result of trusting yourself enough to recognize what you truly deserve. Your power lies in your ability to look within and find clarity—to know that love should reflect the peace and fulfillment you've cultivated, not disrupt it. This is not tied to validation from others; it's the unwavering assurance of being so grounded in your own worth that love becomes an enhancement, not a necessity.

Here's what no one tells you: being the IT Girl in love means refusing to lose yourself in the process. It's the embodiment of showing up as you are—unapologetic and real—and understanding that the right connection will meet you exactly where you stand, never forcing you to bend, twist, or compromise your identity. You don't chase, and you don't negotiate your values for fleeting attention. Instead, it's the unwavering commitment to building a foundation that insists on love as a partnership—one that honors the life you've crafted and the woman you've become. The love you allow into your life should challenge you in the best way, encourage your growth, and align with your deepest truths—without ever making you question your worth or purpose.

Let's be honest: you've seen what happens when people settle for convenience over connection. Maybe you've even been there yourself, trying to force something that felt more like work than love. But you know better now. Love, for you, isn't shaped by compromise in the sense of losing who you are; it's the art of collaboration, of finding someone who matches your energy, your pace, and your vision for life.

The truth? You've outgrown the idea that love should be hard or that it should require proving your worth. You've poured too much into yourself—your growth, your healing, your joy—to let anyone halfway invest in you. Real love isn't a gamble; it's a choice. It's the choice to build something lasting and meaningful with someone who sees your light and only wants to add to it, never dim it. That's the kind of love the IT Girl doesn't just dream of—it's the kind of love she insists on, and nothing less will do.

Embracing Patience: The Art Of Letting Love Unfold

Here's something no one wants to admit: love that's rushed is love that unravels. And the IT Girl knows this better than anyone. She's not interested in flings that burn bright and fade fast or in chasing a connection that's built on convenience instead of compatibility. She's interested in love that grows, deepens, and stands the test of time.

Why Rushing Into Love Does More Harm Than Good:

When you rush, you don't just lose sight of yourself—you lose the chance to truly see the other person. It's so easy to get swept up in the thrill of it all—the late-night calls, the butterflies, the intoxicating feeling of being wanted. The bottom line is this: rushing into love often means you're falling in love with the idea of someone, not who they actually are. Their words might sound great, their gestures might feel grand, but you're skipping the part where trust is built, where actions match words, and where the layers of real compatibility reveal themselves.

You've seen this story before—someone meets someone, dives in headfirst, and suddenly their world tilts off balance. The routines they once cherished fade into the background. Their friendships take a backseat, their dreams get postponed, and their identity begins to shift to fit the mold of what they think their partner wants. The result? A series of compromises so small they seem insignificant in the moment, but they add up. One day, they're staring in the mirror, unsure of the person looking back at them, wondering where the line blurred between who they were and who they've become.

Patience Is Your Superpower

For the IT Girl, patience isn't just a virtue; it's her strongest ally. Patience gives her the space to assess without the pressure of urgency, the wisdom to see beyond surface charm, and the power to trust the quiet signals of her intuition. Love isn't a checklist or a race to the finish line; it's an unfolding story, one that requires time and intention to reveal its true meaning. Rushing through the pages only leaves you skimming the surface of what could be something profound.

Patience is what allows you to truly see someone for who they are—not just their potential or the version of them you hope for, but their reality. It's what gives you the clarity to observe whether their actions align with their words, whether their values resonate with yours, and whether their presence brings more peace than questions. Without patience, love becomes a gamble, a risk of giving your heart to someone whose depths you haven't yet explored.

Think of love as cultivating a garden. The seeds are planted with interest, watered with care, and given time to grow under the right conditions. Rushing the process— overwatering, expecting immediate blooms—only disrupts the beauty that patience could have nurtured. Real love, the kind that sustains and thrives, requires this kind of thoughtful tending. It's slow, steady, and when it finally blossoms, it's breathtaking in its depth and vibrancy.

And what about rushed love? That's like fireworks—a dazzling display that fades almost as quickly as it appeared. It leaves you staring at the sky, longing for something that lasts longer than a fleeting moment. Patience, on the other hand, builds something enduring—a connection that doesn't just survive the seasons but flourishes through them all.

The Power Of Communication Say It Like You Mean It

Here's the IT Girl truth: love without communication is like a ship without a compass—it's bound to get lost. Real connection requires clarity, the kind that strips away pretense and gets to the heart of things. It's not just about saying what's on your mind; it's the quiet strength of being brave enough to speak your truth, even when it feels vulnerable. Because here's the secret: when you communicate openly, you set the tone for the kind of love that thrives on honesty, not assumptions.

Why Communication Is Non-Negotiable

Have you ever found yourself staring at your phone, re-reading a text for the tenth time, trying to decode its hidden meaning? Or maybe you've swallowed your discomfort when something felt off, convincing yourself it wasn't worth the confrontation? Those moments of self-doubt and silence don't just chip away at your peace; they set the tone for a relationship where your needs always come second. That, my dear, is unsustainable.

The IT Girl doesn't operate in ambiguity. If something feels off, she doesn't brush it under the rug. She brings it to the table, lays it out with poise, and seeks clarity. She isn't afraid of hard conversations because she knows they're the cornerstone of trust and intimacy. Difficult conversations aren't obstacles to love; they're the stepping stones to a deeper connection.

How To Communicate Like The IT Girl You Are:

1. **Speak With Certainty:** Before starting a conversation, center yourself. Know that your feelings and boundaries are valid. When you approach a topic, state your truth firmly but kindly. Remember, you're not asking for permission to be understood; you're setting the expectation that your voice deserves space.

2. **Listen Like It Matters:** True communication is a two-way street. While sharing your thoughts is important, give equal weight to your partner's perspective. Ask questions, stay present, and resist the urge to interrupt. Listening doesn't mean agreeing, but it does mean understanding.

3. **Clarify Your Intentions:** Instead of assuming the other person knows what you need, spell it out. For example, say, "I feel disconnected when we don't check in during the day. Can we work on being more intentional about staying in touch?" By being direct, you eliminate confusion and open the door for collaboration.

And here's the truth bomb: if someone consistently resists meeting you at this level of communication, it's not a reflection of your worth—it's a reflection of their limitations. The IT Girl doesn't beg for honesty, respect, or understanding. She exudes it, expects it, and walks away when it's not reciprocated. That's not per; that's self-respect.

Balancing Independence And Togetherness The IT Girl Formula

Let's get one thing crystal clear: you, the IT Girl, are never defined by the role you play in someone else's life. Love, for you, is not about dissolving into someone else's world; it's the art of weaving two lives together in a way that lets both flourish. The kind of relationship you deserve isn't one where you lose yourself—it's the elevation of who you already are.

Why Independence Is Your Ultimate Asset

No one, no matter how amazing, wants the pressure of being someone's everything. That's not love; it's a burden. True connection happens when two whole people come together, not when one person is trying to fill the cracks in the other. Independence is what keeps your spark alive. It's what makes you magnetic, not just to a partner but to yourself. Because you've built a life that's full—a life you're proud of, a life that doesn't need rescuing or rearranging.

Your passions, your friendships, your goals—these aren't extras. They're the foundation. A relationship doesn't replace them; it enhances them. You're not looking for someone to complete you because, darling, you were never incomplete. What you're looking for is someone who sees your brilliance and thinks, "How lucky am I to witness this?"

How To Fiercely Protect Your Independence In Love:

1. **Prioritize Your Passions:** Your career, your hobbies, your ambitions—these aren't negotiable. Make time for the things that make you come alive. Whether it's writing, running a business, or mastering the art of baking the perfect croissant, these are the things that keep you connected to yourself. A partner worth your time will cheer you on, not pull you away from them.

2. **Champion Their Independence:** Here's the secret—the IT Girl knows that independence isn't a one-way street. Just as you need space to grow, so does your partner. Encourage them to pursue their dreams, nurture their own friendships, and cultivate their own happiness. When both people are thriving as individuals, the relationship becomes unshakable.

3. **Claim Your Time Unapologetically:** Alone time isn't selfish; it's essential. Carve out moments just for you—whether it's a weekend spent exploring a new city solo, a quiet evening with a book and a glass of wine, or simply an hour to daydream without interruption. These moments of solitude recharge you and keep you grounded in who you are.

Independence in love has never been about building walls; it's the art of creating a foundation. It's the quiet confidence of showing up as your whole self and expecting nothing less in return. When you honor your individuality, you set the tone for a relationship where both people can shine—together and apart.

Building A Love That Evolves: Growth Is The Goal

Here's the ultimate IT Girl secret: love that lasts isn't static, and it certainly not all about following someone else's blueprint. It's alive, unpredictable, and dynamic. Real love doesn't come with a manual, and that's the beauty of it. It evolves because the people in it evolve, and the IT Girl knows she's not looking for something that fits neatly into a box— she's looking for something real. But when you're stepping into the beginning of a new relationship, this truth can feel both exhilarating and disorienting. It's a dance between vulnerability and discovery, between holding your own and letting someone in.

The beginning of love doesn't seek completeness—it's the art of showing up with all your beautiful complexities and seeing if they meet you there. You're learning their quirks, their dreams, the way they laugh when they're nervous, or the way they pause before they answer a deep question. And, simultaneously, they're learning you: your edges, your rhythms, the things that make you tick. It's uncharted territory, not a performance to master, but an adventure to experience. For you, the IT Girl, the question isn't, "How can I be what they want?" but rather, "Can they walk with me through the path I'm already on?"

The beginning of love isn't fragile—it's ripe with potential. Think of it like tending to a plant you've never grown before. It needs care, attention, and patience, but most importantly, it needs to be nourished in an environment where it can thrive. Love that evolves doesn't happen on autopilot; it requires intention. In those first, electric stages of dating, you're not just evaluating if they're a good fit—you're setting the foundation for a connection that can stand the test of time. Growth is the goal—not completeness, not pretending, but the raw, human process of finding someone who adds to the life you've built and who inspires the life you're still dreaming of.

How To Approach The Early Stages With Grace

Let's start here: the beginning of something new is full of potential, but it's also where illusions can get the best of us. The excitement has a way of sweeping you into a whirlwind of late-night texts and perfectly curated dates, but those dreamy moments can sometimes blur reality. And that's where most people stumble. The infatuation phase tricks them into believing the highlight reel is the whole story. Not you, though. You're the IT Girl. You know better. You know that those first moments—as electric as they are—are just the prologue, not the full narrative. Knowing better means slowing down enough to ensure the story being written is one worth starring in.

Be Intentional About What You're Building

You're not here to audition for a role in someone else's life. You're not adjusting your edges, softening your voice, or dimming your light to fit into a version of what you think they're looking for. Instead, you're showing up as you—fully, unapologetically, and boldly rooted in your truth. The early stages aren't about impressing someone; they're about discovery—yours and theirs.

Here's where you pause to ask yourself the important questions—the ones that go beyond how much you laugh at their jokes or how they look across a candlelit table:

- Does this person's lifestyle align with mine—not just in the present but as I envision my future?

- Do their values not only reflect what I want in a partner but also challenge me to grow?

- Are they bringing clarity to my life, or are they adding noise?

It's tempting to brush off the small warning signs because, let's be real here, chemistry can be intoxicating. But the IT Girl doesn't rely on chemistry alone; she knows that connection without compatibility is like champagne without bubbles—it goes flat fast. You don't settle for surface-level connections. You dig deeper, peeling back the layers of charm to see if there's substance beneath the sparkle. And sometimes, digging deeper means asking yourself the hardest question of all: Am I attracted to them, or am I attracted to the idea of them?

How To Adapt To The Shifts In Dating Dynamics

We all know that the beginning of a relationship is full of shifts. You're navigating how often to text, when to meet each other's friends, and how much to reveal about your past. It's delicate, but it's also an opportunity. The IT Girl knows that this stage is not about playing games or keeping score— it's the art of setting the tone for honest, open communication.

For example, if they're someone who's used to fast-paced flings but you're looking for something meaningful, this is the time to make your intentions clear. You don't have to give them an ultimatum, but you also don't have to mold yourself into what you think they want. Say it like this: "I'm enjoying getting to know you, and I'm looking for something real. What about you?" It's direct, it's confident, and it's exactly what someone worthy of you will respect.

Celebrate The Little Wins

In the early stages, it's not just about seeing if they're right for you—it's also about noticing the small ways they show up. Did they remember your favorite drink? Did they check in after your big meeting? These little gestures matter. They're the building blocks of trust and care.

But here's the flip side: don't let those little gestures make up for a lack of effort in bigger areas. Kind words and sweet moments are lovely, but they're not a substitute for consistency, reliability, or shared values. The IT Girl knows how to appreciate what's good without overlooking what's missing.

Navigating The Balance Between Vulnerability And Strength

Between you and me: letting someone in can feel terrifying, especially when you've been hurt before. Vulnerability can feel like standing in the middle of a crowded room, completely naked, hoping someone won't point out every flaw. But vulnerability isn't weakness; it's strength wrapped in courage. It's the audacity to say, "This is who I am—my edges, my flaws, my scars. Can you meet me here?" It's also the wisdom to say, "If you can't, that's okay, but I'm not about to shrink myself for the sake of being accepted." Vulnerability is where love starts—but only when it's given to someone who's earned it.

The Art Of Vulnerability

We talked about this earlier, but let's revisit it again. Opening up doesn't mean spilling your entire life story like a monologue at a first meeting. Vulnerability is nuanced; it's measured. It's the delicate process of peeling back the layers—slowly, thoughtfully—and giving someone a glimpse of your truth, not the whole novel at once. Think of it as inviting them into your world room by room, rather than handing them the master key.

Here's the secret: vulnerability is less about what you share and more about why and how you share it. Instead of rehashing your most painful breakup on the second date, you might start with, "That experience taught me a lot about how I want to be loved and how I'm capable of loving." That's power. You're not showing them the wound; you're showing them the strength you built because of it.

Let them earn access to the deeper parts of you. Celebrate the things that make you proud first—your quirks, your passions, your talents. Vulnerability isn't tied to laying yourself bare; it's the intentional act of slowly letting someone see the real you, step by step, without losing yourself in the process.

Knowing When To Hold Back

Here's the twist: sometimes, the most vulnerable thing you can do is hold back. There's an undeniable power in restraint—in not rushing to fill silences or oversharing to keep someone interested. Vulnerability, at its best, is a two-way street. If they're pulling back, you let them. If they're not reciprocating your openness, you take a step back and reassess. Vulnerability without reciprocity isn't bravery; it's self-betrayal.

Pay attention to how they handle what you share. Do they listen with care, or do they dismiss it? Do they lean in, or do they retreat? These reactions tell you everything you need to know about whether they're capable of meeting you in the space you're creating. And if they can't? That's not a reflection of your worth—it's a sign that they're not ready for the kind of depth you bring.

True vulnerability thrives in balance. It requires giving enough to create connection while keeping enough for yourself to maintain your dignity. It means trusting your instincts when something feels off and having the courage to say, *"I deserve more than half-measures."* In love, the IT Girl knows: vulnerability doesn't require throwing open the doors to your heart for just anyone; it demands discernment—deciding who gets the key, and when.

So, you've met someone new, and the spark is there. What now?

You, the IT Girl, don't just sit back and hope for the best. You set the tone. You show up with intention. You balance vulnerability with discernment. And most importantly, you keep your standards high—because the right person won't just meet them; they'll exceed them.

Now that you are at here, it's time for me to ask you again after reading this book...

Who are you? Who do you say you are? Who are you identifying as?

_____

_____

_____

_____

_____

_____

_____

_____

_____

_____

_____

_____

_____

_____

_____

_____

_____

_____

_____

_____

_____

_____

_____

_____

_____

_____

Here we are, darling. The final page, the last word—but let's not call this an ending. Let's call it a new beginning. You, the IT Girl, have traveled through the trenches of heartbreak, stood in front of the mirror and seen yourself anew, and stitched together the pieces of your heart with threads of wisdom, resilience, and grace. You've done what so many fear: you've faced yourself. And now, you're stepping into the world of love not as someone waiting to be chosen, but as someone who has already chosen herself.

This journey wasn't just about finding love—it was about finding *you*. About remembering that the love you give yourself is the blueprint for every other love you'll allow in. You've learned to hold your standards high, to let go of what doesn't serve you, and to embrace the vulnerability that comes with saying, "I am worthy, as I am."

As you turn the page into your next chapter, know this: the love you deserve isn't out of reach. It's already circling you, drawn to the light you've cultivated within. Whether it's a quiet moment of joy in your own company, a connection that feels like home, or a love story that evolves in ways you never expected—trust that it's coming. And trust that you are ready for it.

Love, as you now know, is not the destination. It's the journey. It's the moments you laughed too hard at dinner, the times you walked away from what wasn't meant for you, and the quiet victories of learning to let someone in without losing yourself. It's every little choice you make to honor your heart, to keep growing, and to stay open to what's possible.

So, what's next for you, IT Girl? Maybe it's a first date (or dates) that surprises you. Maybe it's a love so rich and deep it feels like a second skin. Or maybe, for now, it's the sweet solitude of a Sunday morning spent in your own company, knowing that you are enough. Whatever it is, trust that you are ready. You are whole. And you are more than enough. You are love.

You've learned that heartbreak doesn't break you; it refines you. You've discovered that knowing yourself is the greatest love story of all, and you've stepped into a place of confidence, clarity, and power. Now, as you step into the world of dating and love, remember this: you are the writer of your own story. You get to choose who earns a place in your narrative, and you get to decide what kind of love is worth your time and your heart.

The Declarations

The Declarations

In the next few pages, you will discover a powerful declaration. These declarations are designed to help you reflect, reinforce, and embody the truths they represent. To get the most out of them, start by reading each declaration aloud to yourself and letting the words sink in. You can revisit them anytime, making this a personal ritual that strengthens your self-love and mindset with every read.

Love Flows When I Show Up For Myself First.

I Am My Favorite Person.

You Deserve Flowers, Love Letters, And Pure, Passionate Love.

Heal And
Never Go Back.

Make Yourself
The Priority.

This Blessing Is Proof That God Is With You.

I Am Choosing Me Every Time.

I Told Myself, 'I'm Too Pretty For This,' And Then I Moved On.

Thank You God.

I Know Things Will Work Out Better Than I Imagined.

Made in the USA
Columbia, SC
11 May 2025

57662926R00187